RATE OF CLIMB

RATE OF CLIMB

THRILLING PERSONAL REMINISCENCES
FROM A FIGHTER PILOT AND LEADER

To Ken,
Enjoy my story.
With Best Wishes

Rick Peacock-Edwards

AIR COMMODORE RICK
PEACOCK-EDWARDS CBE, AFC

GRUB STREET • LONDON

Published by
Grub Street
4 Rainham Close
London SW11 6SS

A CIP record for this title is available from the British library

ISBN-13: 978-1-911621-46-1

Printed and bound by Finidr, Czech Republic

CONTENTS

DEDICATION

This book is dedicated to my widely travelled family in the UK and South Africa, to my flying colleagues and, especially, to my valued friends who were killed in flying accidents during my Royal Air Force career and who, therefore, are unable to read this book. In particular, I wish to remember:

- **Trevor Sharp**, a member of my pre-Lightning flying course at RAF Chivenor. Trevor was killed in a Hunter flying accident in 1967.

- **Jerry Bowler**, whom I served with on No. 92 Squadron flying Lightnings at RAF Gütersloh, Germany. Jerry was killed in a Gnat flying accident in 1969, whilst a member of the Red Arrows RAF aerobatic display team.

- **Colin Armstrong**, with whom I also served on No. 92 Squadron flying Lightnings at RAF Gütersloh. Colin was killed in a Gnat mid-air collision in 1971, whilst a member of the Red Arrows.

- **Graham Ivell**, with whom I served on No. 92 Squadron flying Lightnings and who was killed along with three other good friends: David Kiefer (United States Air Force exchange officer), Ian Sanford and Dave Mather, in a mid-air collision between two Gnats whilst qualified flying instructors at RAF Valley in 1976.

- **John Grzybowski**, killed in a Gnat flying accident at RAF Shawbury in October 1976.

- **David Haward**, a fellow flying instructor on the Gnat at RAF Valley killed in a Harrier accident whilst Officer Commanding RAF Wittering.

- **Terry Bushnell, Taff Hinchcliff and John Rigby**, ex-Lightning pilots, all killed flying Jaguars.

- **Frank Whitehouse and Pete Thompson**, killed whilst flying Lightnings on No. 74 Squadron in Singapore.

- **P V Lloyd**, a fellow qualified flying instructor at RAF Valley, killed in a Jaguar in 1989.

- **John Armitage**, my cousin, an outstanding officer, killed in a Canberra flying accident at RAF Wyton in May 1977.

- **Chris Jones and Mike Stephenson**, killed on a night-flying sortie in 1978 at RAF Leuchars whilst we were serving on No. 111 Squadron flying Phantoms. Chris had formerly flown Lightnings. His wife Dorothy is godmother to my daughter, Jenny.

- **Josh Tallantyre** (United States Air Force exchange officer) and Chris Ferris, killed flying at RAF Leuchars in 1978 whilst we served on No. 111 Squadron flying Phantoms.

- **Steve Roncoroni**, a fellow student at RAF Acklington during our flying training, killed in a Shackleton in 1990.

- **Guy Bancroft-Wilson**, fellow instructor at RAF Valley and ex-Red Arrows pilot, killed in a Bell P-63 Kingcobra during a Biggin Hill Warbirds air display in 2001.

- **Ken Hayr**, a New Zealander, and my respected commander as the Air Officer Commanding No. 11 Fighter Group; killed in a de Havilland Vampire during an air display at Biggin Hill in 2001.

- **Jack Thompson**, who had served with me on No. 111 Squadron. He was killed in a flying accident at RAF Abingdon during a practice display in preparation for the Abingdon Air Display in 1988.

- **Mike Blee**, fellow pilot on No. 6 Air Experience Flight at RAF Benson, killed in a mid-air collision with a glider whilst flying the Grob G 115 Tutor in 2009.

FOREWORD

Rick Peacock-Edwards has been a great friend since the heady days when we were both flying the Lightning, and our paths have crossed frequently throughout our respective careers in the Royal Air Force. (Both No. 11 Group commanders at the same time in our careers.) Rick has seen more than most in his aviation career both inside and outside of the service and this book brings those experiences into sharp relief. The son of a Battle of Britain pilot, flying was obviously in his veins from a very young age, and from his early education in South Africa to joining the RAF one can already see the drive that eventually took him to high rank. Indeed, he followed the classic fighter pilot path – always striving for excellence when in the cockpit, and never far from trouble when out.

Importantly, as you move through his career, in such iconic aircraft as the Lightning, Gnat, Phantom and Tornado, Rick has highlighted candidly not only the wonderful camaraderie and fun that we all had, but the stresses and strains that inevitably beset any large organisation. As a flying instructor, flight commander, squadron commander and then station commander he is very well equipped to reflect on the Royal Air Force of the day – and its readiness to meet the demands of conflict. When wrestled out of a cockpit – which was never for long – his staff appointments were no less demanding and the reader will get a straightforward and sometimes blunt look at the machinery that kept the Royal Air Force operational.

Latterly, he took up the position of Inspector of Flight Safety for the RAF, an independent position in which he reported directly to the chief of the Air Staff. This vitally important position laid responsibility on him for the overall safety protocols and mechanisms that allowed the RAF to complete the operational mission in the safest manner possible. Many would have treated operations and safety as mutually incompatible, but Rick managed to move forward both very effectively in his normal pragmatic fashion. His involvement with flight safety opened many doors such that many years after his retirement he is still very active in the promotion and management of aviation safety. Indeed, his post-RAF career has been, in many ways, no less interesting than his time in the service. He has filled director and managing director positions, he had a very successful year as Master of the Honourable Company of Air Pilots and still in 2019 he is patron, president, chairman or vice chairman of a dozen or so organisations. In particular, I know that he takes great pleasure from his association with the RAF Club in London and his involvement with air displays.

However, a short foreword cannot do full justice to the breadth and scope of the very many activities and positions in which Rick Peacock-Edwards has been involved. Suffice to say, he brings much colour to all of these activities – as much as you will gain from reading about the spills and thrills of flying some of the most exciting aircraft of his generation.

Air Marshal Cliff Spink CB CBE FCMI FRAeS

INTRODUCTION
MY FATHER'S WARTIME EXPLOITS

My father, Spencer Ritchie Peacock-Edwards, known as 'Teddy', was born in Kokstad on 27th May 1915. He later attended Michaelhouse in Natal, South Africa. He was one of 11 candidates selected in Southern Rhodesia by a Royal Air Force Board to join the RAF on a short-service commission. He sailed to the UK and began initial training on 7th March 1938. Posted to 2FTS Brize Norton on 21st May and, with training completed, he joined No. 150 Squadron Boscombe Down on 17th December in the same year, equipped with three-seat Fairey Battles. Pilots of the light bomber found themselves flying in an obsolete deathtrap, no match for the superior Luftwaffe. Squadron losses were catastrophic.

The squadron flew to France on 2nd September 1939 and my father was detached to Boscombe Down for a short gunnery course (8th-17th October). In June 1940, the squadron was evacuated from France and returned to the UK where he volunteered to serve with Dowding's Fighter Command and on 3rd September he was posted to No. 615 Squadron at Prestwick to convert to the Hurricane.

He moved to No. 253 Squadron, based at Kenley, on 13th September and on 6th October possibly destroyed a Do17 (unrecorded). On the 21st he damaged a Do17, and on the 30th was credited with damaging 'the most dangerous enemy', a Me109; on 22nd November he damaged another Do17 and on 3rd December shared in the destruction of a further Do17.

On 15th December, destined for the Middle East, he embarked on the aircraft carrier HMS *Furious* via Liverpool, flying a Hurricane off at Takoradi on 9th January 1941. In company with fellow pilots, he flew a Hurricane north on the multi-stage ferry routed to Ismailia, Egypt, from where he flew in a Sunderland to Malta, arriving 30th January.

Joining No. 261 Squadron at Hal Far, he claimed a Ju88 destroyed on 1st February, was appointed 'A' Flight commander on the 16th, accounting for two Ju87s, and damaging another on 23rd March. He destroyed a Me109 on

13th April and then made a forced crash-landing in his stricken Hurricane, V7472. In May 1941 he returned to the Middle East theatre, and from August instructed at Gordon's Tree OTU, Sudan. Later that year he joined the Pilot Pool, Kasfareet.

In February 1942 he embarked on HMS *Indomitable*, taking off at Ceylon on 7th March to join 'G' Squadron (renumbered 258 on 30th March). The squadron was scrambled on Easter Sunday 5th April when Japanese carrier-based aircraft attacked Colombo. He is credited with destroying an enemy naval aircraft and probably a Zero. However, for the second time during the war he was forced to crash-land his Hurricane in a paddy field and walked away with only minor injuries. Years later I met the Japanese pilot credited with shooting down my father. He wished to atone for what happened in the war and it was a memorable and moving meeting which attracted much media interest at the time. Posted to No. 273 Squadron, Katukurunda, in August 1942, my father was awarded the DFC (gazetted 29th December 1942) for his achievements during the Easter Sunday battles.

He had been at sea set on course for Singapore when it fell to the Japanese oppressor and that is why he then ended up in Ceylon, then a British Crown Colony. But for this diversion he would not have met my mother, Gillian (known as Jill) Sheila Armitage, whom he married on 9th January 1943 in Ceylon. She was the daughter of a British tea planter; generations of the family had run a tea estate in Ceylon known as 'Frocroft'. My mother was educated in the UK and only saw her parents when they came to the UK which was not very often. Unlike today, there was little capability to return to Ceylon for the school holidays. It must have been hard for my mother and her twin brother, Jack, one of my godfathers. They used to go to a holiday home during the school holidays run by Reverend Hayes and his wife. I know my mother enjoyed her time with this family who were very kind and loving. One of the sons of Reverend Hayes, Murray, was the other of my two godfathers. He was always very good to me throughout his life and we had much in common, namely flying and a military background. Murray had been a pilot and commander in the Royal Navy.

By February 1943 my father was commanding No. 30 Squadron, equipped with Hurricanes, in Colombo, leading it until April 1944, when he returned to the UK. After the war, the family, that is my parents plus me and my brother, John, returned briefly to Southern Rhodesia in 1946 before my father then returned to the RAF in 1947. He finally retired from the RAF on 14th February 1958 with the rank of squadron leader, and we returned to live permanently in South Africa. My father died in September 1983 and my mother in May 2007.

So, why, you may ask, am I telling you so much about my parents. My father and his fellow Battle of Britain pilots were my heroes as a child and remain my heroes to this day. Their way of life has driven my way of life and continues to do so, and I feel that telling you about my father's flying career/exploits will help you understand my own feelings. My mother, likewise, was a very beautiful and lively lady, and incredibly loving. She also liked a good party and has equally played a major and influential part in my life.

CHAPTER ONE
EARLY YEARS IN THE UK

My family can date their ancestral origins to the north of the border, where my forebears still retain a family law practice in Edinburgh. Connections with South Africa began when my grandfather fought in the Boer War and stayed on in the country. My grandfather farmed initially in East Griqualand and later at a very large farm called Broadwell in the Plumtree area, Southern Rhodesia.

My father had an elder sister, Judy, who for most of her life lived in Rhodesia (now Zimbabwe) but moved south to Howick in South Africa with her husband, John, when the Zimbabwe problems started to develop. They were not able to take with them many of their possessions and none of any wealth. They had three children; Anne, who lives in Johannesburg; Christopher, a vet, and who still lives in Zimbabwe; and Margaret who lives in Northumberland. Judy was my godmother, and a very good one too, and it was she who helped to develop my lifelong interest in stamp collecting – she used to send me all the first day covers when new stamps were introduced in Rhodesia.

My mother had a twin brother, Jack Armitage, who definitely had an influence on my life. I was told that he and I were very similar both in looks and character. He was a great party-lover. He was one of my two godfathers and I have always had the greatest respect for him as a really good chap. His first wife, Audrey, was my favourite aunt. She and Jack had two children, John and Kay, who themselves started life in Ceylon where Jack was the sixth or seventh generation to run the family tea estate. I see a lot of Kay to this day and John followed me into the RAF as a pilot. Unfortunately, his very promising career was cruelly cut short when he was killed in a Canberra flying accident on 3rd May 1977. He too is greatly missed. I can well remember being told, when others discovered that John was a relative, 'John Armitage is your cousin but he is so couth, how can he be your cousin?' I am not sure how to take that one. My other cousin, Kay, who I gave away at her wedding in September 1977, lives very close to me in Berkshire and I am godfather to her son, John.

> 'Richard really is a model baby, always happy and contented. He adores his bath and kicks and splashes the water, making the nursery floor look like a miniature flood. He is a perfect picture of babyhood.'

The above is a quotation from my nanny's diary. She looked after me and my two brothers, John and Michael. She was a highly qualified, English and very professional lady. A caring and lovely person whom the three of us remembered with great affection. She was very much a part of the family and she also had an excellent rapport with my parents. She stayed with the family through time spent in the UK, South Africa and Southern Rhodesia until I was about five or six. After she left, we remained in close touch and the last time that we met was in 1982 when my son, Ian, was christened (in the same robes in which I was christened). She died shortly after that event. However, in 2015 an amazing coincidence happened.

A very good friend of mine who was Lieutenant Governor of Guernsey, Air Marshal Peter Walker, very sadly and suddenly died, aged just 65. I went to his funeral in the RAF Church St. Clement Danes and then to the reception at the RAF Club afterwards in Piccadilly, where there was a package waiting for me.

I picked it up but did not open it until I got home and in it was a book. First of all, there was a note from the office of His Excellency the Lieutenant Governor of Guernsey, then there was a letter from this lady who obviously had the same nanny as me, as did her mother. She lived in Guernsey, knew Peter Walker and asked if he knew me, he did (we were good friends) and asked if he could convey the diary. Very sadly he was unable to deliver the diary personally but his wife Linda left it for me at the club. I opened it and what a surprise. It was really the story of my first six months in this world in a report kept by my nanny. It was the first time that I even knew that the diary existed, at age 70. The world is full of surprises!

All I can say is that 'I was the perfect baby', or at least that is the way I was described. Actually, my mother always used to tell me that I was a very good child until I was about eight.

I am the eldest of three brothers, with an age difference of three-and-a-quarter years between us. We were always close, very close, and have been throughout our lives. My middle brother, John (known as Johnny), is 15 months younger than me, and like me, he was educated at Michaelhouse and went on to attend the University of the Witwatersrand in Johannesburg. As I have already said, Johnny and I were close, but there was always a love-hate relationship that existed between us, and at times we fought like hell, often arguing for the sake of arguing, particularly when our wives were present. They would ask "what are you two arguing about? You are saying exactly the same thing!" In a bit of a roller coaster life, John was always an entrepreneur. In this capacity, he sometimes took risks, he made money and he lost money. He passed away in 2015 and he is missed. He was a dedicated family man who loved life and people and he was well supported by his lovely wife, Fran, herself the daughter of another Ceylon tea planter. They have three daughters.

Michael, known as Mike, is my youngest brother, two years younger than John. He too attended Michaelhouse and went on to Natal University to study economics. Mike, after spending most of his working life in Johannesburg, now lives in the Cape with his wife, Di. He is a solid character who learned much from the mistakes of his two elder brothers. He retired as the chief executive of the South African Forestry Association. Mike has a son and daughter from his first marriage to Bobby, plus a stepson, James.

We boys had a very happy family life and, from my perspective, an upbringing that can be divided into two phases, one in the UK and the other in South Africa. Until I was aged 12, we seemed to be moving house often, especially whilst my father was still serving in the RAF. I was born in Maidstone on 27th January 1945 when my parents were living in Kent. My brother, John, was also born in Maidstone. By the time I was two years old we had lived in both the UK and Southern Rhodesia. We had travelled to and from South Africa by Union Castle ship, the *Athlone Castle* I recall. I do not remember anything from this period in my life apart from a vague memory of going up Table Mountain in Cape Town in a cable car. I must then have been aged two and we must have been on our way back to the UK.

On our return from Africa in 1947 we first lived in a village near Bournemouth where my brother, Mike, was born. I can remember rabbits in the garden where we lived but that is about all. I think it must have been in late 1948 that we moved to a lovely house in Iver, Bucks called 'The Beeches'. It was from this time onwards that my memory becomes clearer. The Beeches was the first of two houses that we lived in in Iver, the second was called 'The Homestead' which I remember as not being as nice as The Beeches. John and I were absolute tearabouts on our tricycles and treated them like go-karts; we were dangerous and no more so than when Mike, just walking, also wanted to play. I am afraid that he did not get much sympathy from his elder brothers.

It was whilst living at Iver that John and I went to our first school, Westfield, which was very close to where we lived. I enjoyed my time there but I am not so sure about John – he played truant on a number of occasions. I also remember being asked to take John home on his first day at school because he had wet his trousers, obviously a traumatic experience and I hasten to add that that was the only time. One of the other things that I remember about our time in Iver was spending a lot of time visiting the farm at the bottom of the road, run by a lovely family called the Judds. Their lifestyle really attracted my interest and I immediately felt a great love for both nature and the countryside. Haystacks were a great attraction to play in and around, happy days.

I also used to help the milkman from United Dairies every morning with his milk round. It meant a very early start but I did not mind that and I was getting paid sixpence per round. I remember well how rich I felt when I had amassed 19 shillings but that amount of money could go a long way in those days. I also remember how I used to go and watch trains and, in particular, the great steam trains that operated on the Great Western railway line, a fabulous sight. I was a train spotter and I noted the numbers of every train.

I remember a bonfire in the garden and seeing a Johnson's baby powder tin in the fire. Why do I remember this, because I tried to pluck the tin from the fire, what a silly boy. I badly burnt my hand but lesson learned! Finally, I can remember going with the family to visit some good friends who lived nearby, an army brigadier called Crowdy, and his family. I ended up in disgrace when I let his birds out of their cage, never to be seen again.

I went on from nursery to a prep school called Long Close in Upton Road, Slough. The school was housed in a very large old house with views towards Windsor Castle. Initially, I went as a day boy but not for very long because my parents moved to Wilmslow in Cheshire and I became a boarder for the first time at just seven years old. John had joined me at Long Close by this time and he was boarding at age six. There weren't many boarders at the school and we all lived in one dormitory. I remember pillow fights, walks to church on Sundays and playing in the grounds of the school, in particular at weekends. In the summer there was a nice swimming pool to occupy our time. By the time I was seven, I had become an accomplished swimmer and I was winning everything, at both swimming and diving. However, one weekend I dived into the swimming pool at Long Close and hit my head on the bottom of the pool. Apart from giving me a big shock, and I can't remember whether or not I knocked myself out, for a number of years after that event I lost my nerve when it came to diving, with the notable exception of doing racing dives at the start of swimming races. I remained unbeatable in the pool.

I remember being generally happy at Long Close but I also remember feeling homesick at the start of each term – school is not the same as home. John was the same and I know that my mother found it all a very traumatic experience, she always hated her boys being away from home.

Holiday time was also very special, always, and not just because we were at home but also because, usually, several times per year, we would go to Jersey where my maternal grandparents lived. My grandmother came from a Jersey family called Ogier and was one of 13 children, many of whom lived until they were over 100 years old. I loved our holidays in Jersey and I still have a deep love for the island, the beaches, the lovely coves, Jersey cows, new potatoes, everything. It was sad when my grandfather suddenly died but my grandmother then lived in a large apartment in St Helier, Number 45 The Esplanade, overlooking St Aubins Bay, Elizabeth Castle, the harbour – the views were fantastic. My brothers and I used to watch for the daily mail ship to appear round Corbiere Point and then we would all race down to the entrance of the harbour, arriving just as the ship was coming through the entrance. We would then watch passenger disembarkation and the unloading of freight. The harbour was a fascinating place and we used to spend many hours just looking at all the busy activity. There was so much to see and it was all so new and fascinating.

My grandmother was a very special person, very kind to us boys. In particular, we used to love the cream teas that she would buy for us when we visited the biggest shop in St Helier called Voisins. The Voisin family were also our relations! My grandmother also used to make the most delicious fudge. I used to enjoy the dizzy feeling that I got from eating the fudge, it gave me a real kick!

Most summers we would spend the whole holiday on Jersey, the island became like a second home. I also remember learning all about the German occupation during World War II which, of course, affected the lives of most of my grandmother's family. How the islanders must have suffered. Whilst we were in Jersey my father used to spend much of the time at work back on the mainland but he would regularly fly a Chipmunk to the island for weekends and I can well remember the excitement of going to meet him at Jersey airport. He would also take a few weeks' leave to be with his family.

During our time living in Wilmslow we lived in an officers' married quarter on the RAF base there but because John and I were away most of the year at boarding school, and in the school holidays we were so often in Jersey, we were not there very much. However, I do remember one occasion when we had been playing down near the railway line. John, in particular, was a bit of a troublemaker and on this occasion he had set fire to the grass embankment by the rail track. This led to the fire service being called and a pretty severe ticking off for both of us at home, me because I was the eldest and should have been able to stop John. Some hope, if you knew my brother you would know that he very much had a mind of his own, all of his life.

After a few years at Wilmslow my father was posted to the Air Ministry in London and we moved to Leeds Village in Kent where my parents bought a lovely house in the village, 'Willow Tree House'. The house was on the outskirts of the village, opposite the church. It was also only a short walk to the village shops, in particular a sweet shop owned, as I recall, by a lady called Tuck. Very appropriate. There was also a butcher and I remember on a number of occasions our pet dachshund sneaking into the shop only to re-emerge with a string of sausages in his mouth followed by an irate butcher. Also worthy of mention, my parents bought the house from the family of a famous test pilot, Mike Lithgow, who very sadly was killed whilst flight testing a commercial BAC 111 prototype in 1963. Yet another aviation connection in my life!

We lived in Leeds Village for about four years and these were some of the happiest years of my life – it was bliss to live in such an idyllic village and English countryside environment. The house itself had a lot of space and six or seven bedrooms, and a very large garden. Also, for probably the first time, I had my own bedroom. During my time at Willow Tree House I spent a lot of time in the countryside and developed a deep love for nature. Spring was always a special season to me because everything was so new and fresh plus it signalled the end of what in those days seemed to be long, hard winters. I used to enjoy looking for birds' nests in the hedgerows and I used to love watching the birds (the feathered variety, the other variety came later). I also had a menagerie of pets. My father created an aviary for me in the summer house where I bred budgerigars and one or two other exotic birds. I bought two mice and started to breed them. I was heartbroken when the female mouse produced one baby but as I opened the cage our cat pounced and that was the end of that baby mouse. However, it was not long before a litter of four or five mice was produced and in no time at all I had many, many mice, so many in fact that my father banished me with the mice to the attic. When we finally left Willow Tree House my father had to call in the rat catcher to catch the mice that had escaped and were now running around loose in the attic. I was as popular as ever! I also had two tortoises.

Around the back of Willow Tree House was an ideal piece of land for a cricket net. My father generously provided the net and us boys used to spend as much time as possible practising cricket in the net. The three of us were cricket mad and played for the school teams. At that time we had severe aspirations to become test cricketers. We also had a snooker table in the house and so our home lives were nothing but competitive, and at times combative.

Another major event that came with our move to Kent was that John and I left Long Close School and went as day boys to a lovely little prep school, Eylesden Court, which was situated on the Green in the delightful village of Bearsted. I very much enjoyed Eylesden Court and I must have been there for two to three years before I moved on to my first public school. I just remember our time in Leeds with warmth and affection, we were at good schools and at the same time able to enjoy the fruits of an excellent home life. My mother's cooking, in particular, was always very special. She was a Cordon Bleu cook and her meals were excellent. I am afraid, as my wife, Tina, knows, I have never forgotten the excellence of my mother's cooking. especially her scrambled eggs. The parties were also pretty good at Willow Tree House!

At Eylesden Court I entered into the full life of the school and did very well. I played a lot of sport and participated in as many activities as I could. I made many friends including Howard, who was the son of the famous England cricket wicket keeper Godfrey Evans, whom my parents got to know well. I also remember one event which caused a problem for the school. Whilst I had been at Long Close there was a master there who was removed from the teaching staff. I was very surprised to see this same master join the staff at Eylesden Court. I always remembered him because he used to talk about how he had milked seals in Antarctica. He was a real Walter Mitty person. Anyway, I told my parents who then must have spoken to the headmaster, a nice man called Fortescue-Thomas. He obviously carried out some investigative work and in no time at all this same master disappeared from the scene just as quickly as he had arrived.

Also, whilst at Eylesden Court I sat the 11+ examination and, amazingly to me, I passed with flying colours and was awarded a major scholarship to Sutton Valence School, an old English public school (founded 1596) in Kent. My place was totally free, it didn't cost my parents one penny. Needless to say, my parents were delighted, as was I, and in September 1956 I began the next, what turned out to be short, chapter in my schooling life.

Sutton Valence was predominantly a boarding school although there were a number of day boys, of which I was one, who were placed in the Day Boys House, Founders. I remember the house master as a nice, friendly man called Craven. In those days, there were around 400 boys at the school. The school itself had magnificent buildings and was situated on the top of a hill with commanding views over the Kent countryside; it was an impressive place. I had a very happy 15 months at Sutton Valence before my parents decided that it was time for the family to return to South Africa.

At school, I enjoyed the classwork but not the homework. I used to cycle to and from Leeds to the school and when I got home, usually in the early evening, I always wanted to be doing other things rather than work. I guess I was a bit lazy as far as work was concerned and I recall telling some real porkies to my mother about having done my prep! I greatly enjoyed all sports and excelled, in particular, in the swimming pool where I swam freestyle and backstroke and was the champion in my year. I still retained my fear of diving and when I was told that if I had dived as well that I would have won the ultimate trophy, the Victor Ludorum, I knew that I had to overcome my fear of diving and this I progressively did over the next few years. I was also a member of the Scouts and used to love all the opportunities to learn practical things and skills in the outdoors.

In late 1957 my father told me that I was going to have to leave Sutton Valence because we were moving to South Africa. I was not happy and that is putting it mildly. I had settled very well at Sutton Valence and, quite simply, I did not want to leave either my school or my friends. I recall that I was not shy in telling my parents what I thought but all to no avail. I had made a lot of friends; I loved my school and I loved living in our house in Leeds Village. The last thing that I wanted to do was to give all that up. Also, I was now aged 12 and at a very critical age, as I have, since, often surmised.

My best friend at Sutton Valence was a chap in my year called Christopher Byng-Maddick. We had previously attended prep school together and so had known each other for some time and our parents were friends. His parents owned a farm not too far from Sutton Valence and I can remember very happy times on the farm. We lost contact when we left the UK but some years ago, I was delighted when I received a friend request from him on Facebook. We have since re-established contact and periodically meet in London for a beer or two. He became an architect and I have found it fascinating to fill in all the gaps after so many years. Our friendship remains strong. And I still remain in good contact with Sutton Valence, I attend Old Suttonian functions in London and I have also been their guest speaker on several occasions.

CHAPTER 2
GROWING UP IN SOUTH AFRICA

I found leaving the UK to return once again to South Africa, at age 12, a considerable wrench but at least we had a marvellous two weeks, in January 1958, travelling by ship between Southampton and Cape Town, with a stop at Madeira on the way. This provided time to transition and for me to settle my thoughts. My brothers and I very much enjoyed the voyage on board one of the Union Castle liners, I think it was the *Windsor Castle*. I was fascinated by all that happened on board; the ship, the uniforms of the officers, the excellent food, the fellow passengers and, in particular, the daily sweep that took place to guess the number of miles travelled over the previous 24 hours. I also thoroughly enjoyed the 'crossing the line' ceremony as we crossed the equator. All in all, it was an enjoyable experience on the way to what, to me, seemed like the great unknown even though I knew that I had already lived in Africa, but I had been just too young to remember.

We arrived in Cape Town in mid-January 1958, about two weeks before I was planned to start at my new school, Michaelhouse, where my father had also previously been educated over 30 years earlier. I was sad to say goodbye to our ship and we no sooner had docked than we were off the ship and on a train heading from Cape Town to Johannesburg, a distance of about 1,000 miles. The train journey, as I recall, took one day and two nights and took us through scenery which was very different from the lush green countryside in England. There were magnificent mountains and semi-arid desert and where there were the villages, we seemed to only periodically come across places of human habitation.

We were met in Johannesburg by my father's very good friend, Geoff Ross. They knew each other from my father's time living in Southern Rhodesia and they had both worked with the Rhodesian railways before my father joined the RAF in 1938. We moved into a flat in a suburb in the northern suburbs of Johannesburg called Illovo, very different from the spacious house that we had lived in in Kent. The next ten days were spent getting myself and my brothers kitted out and ready to start at our new schools at the end of January. Term times in South Africa were very different from the UK, mainly because the seasons happen at different times of the year but also because our new schools were four terms per year and thus far we had attended schools with three terms per year. Whilst I was going to Michaelhouse, John and Mike were going as boarders to Cordwalles School in Pietermaritzburg, Natal, very much a feeder prep school for Michaelhouse. I also remember a dental appointment in those first two weeks in South Africa. I had had some tooth problems on the ship and I ended up having six teeth removed, baby teeth that should have already gone!

The day approached when I was due to start at Michaelhouse and I was not looking forward to it at all. I knew nothing about the school and I knew only one person who was also about to go to Michaelhouse and who would be in the same house, Pascoe. My parents had been introduced to his parents and this led to me being introduced to Sandy Berry. He remained a good friend both at school and afterwards. He sadly passed away at a young age.

Prior to being taken to Michaelhouse by my parents we drove from Johannesburg to Durban in the new family car, a small Vauxhall. We stayed in a lovely hotel in Umhlanga Rocks called The Oyster Box and we enjoyed a very pleasant few days of luxury before progressing to the 'great unknown'.

The day finally came and we drove from Durban to the village of Balgowan in the Natal Midlands where Michaelhouse was located. The countryside was very beautiful and much more like that in Scotland, and it was green. I felt much happier but I was still full of trepidation.

Michaelhouse is very much the Eton of South Africa and it really is a quite magnificent school, situated in an idyllic setting in the Natal countryside and not far from the Drakensberg Mountain range with mountains that rose up to 10,000 feet. The facilities at the school were excellent, especially the sporting facilities. The school had been very much modelled on an English public school and, in particular, a school like Gordonstoun, or so we were led to believe. It had first been founded in Pietermaritzburg in 1896. In 1958, there were 400 boys at the school, all boarders, and we were accommodated in seven houses. My house, Pascoe, was the newest house. My housemaster was also the deputy rector (headmaster), a powerful man in every way, called Tommy Norwood. He had been educated at Fettes in Scotland and he had also played rugby for Scotland. Years later my parents, who were very friendly with Tommy and his wife, told me that he had once said to them that he understand every boy in the school but the one boy that he could not understand was, guess who, me. Oh well!

The dormitories in Pascoe were interlinked with no doors between them and each dormitory segment accommodated 12 boys. There was little privacy anywhere including when you went to the toilet, we were not allowed to even close lavatory doors, it was all very public. The way of life at the school started at six a.m. when the wake-up bell would ring. A cold shower, or plunge in those houses with a plunge pool, was compulsory and roll call followed at six thirty. We had two lessons before breakfast and then lessons all morning. Lunch was followed by a quiet period on our beds before sport on every afternoon. After sport there was time for extracurricular activities such as carpentry, apart from two days per week (Tuesday and Thursday) when we would have two lessons before dinner. There were also lessons on Saturday mornings. Prep periods followed in the evenings and lights out was at nine p.m. I certainly found it all very strange for some considerable time but I gradually got used to my new environment and my new school regime.

In my first two weeks at Michaelhouse we had mentors to help us find our way around the school and who were also supposed to help to educate us about the history of the school. In our first year we were known as 'cacks' and we used to fag for the prefects. I remember my mentor, a boy in the year above me, I will not mention his name but who, as far as I was concerned, was an absolute s**t. He was an unpleasant bully. I will never forget him shutting my fingers under the lid of a school desk and the mental abuse that he inflicted on this new boy who had come from an English school. It was certainly not the way I had wanted to start at my new school and I will never forget him and his unpleasantness towards me in those first two weeks at Michaelhouse. That, fortunately, was most definitely the low point during my time at Michaelhouse. The large majority of boys at the school were very nice indeed and many of them remain personal friends to this day. However, there is also no doubt that it took me a long time to settle down in my new environment but as time went by I grew to like the school more and more and to this day I am very grateful for the rounded education that it gave me during my four years as a pupil. During my transition from the UK to South Africa I was at a vulnerable age when my life changed and, whilst it was not easy at the time, and I don't think that my parents ever really knew the depth of the trauma that I was experiencing, my time there was helping form my character. I was learning a lot about myself and, in particular, that I have considerable inner strength and that I am not a quitter, and I know that I am a better person for the experience. My father was a great one for the use of phrases and the relevant one for my development is aptly summed up by his use of the dictum 'out of adversity comes strength'. That is just so true.

Michaelhouse was a tough school and it certainly 'maketh you a man'. I have a lot of happy memories of my time there, the excellence of the teaching and the high quality of the staff, the sport, the camaraderie, the considerable opportunities in so many directions. The facilities were quite the best that I have ever seen in any school and that remains the case to this day.

On Sundays, we were not allowed to remain within the school boundary for much of the day, or put another way we had to go out into the countryside and, basically, fend for ourselves. We were given a packed lunch. It was another great way of finding out more about the environment around you, and getting to know others in your year group better. We had to go out in groups for safety reasons. There was a range of things to do, from catching snakes to finding a place to swim, chat and eat, and sometimes smoke, to climbing the large hill that overlooked the school called Beacon Hill, and much more. Sadly, I remember one Sunday when we were by a river and we all got involved in a bit of a mud fight using self-made catapults to launch mud balls at each other across the stream. Unfortunately, one of the chaps in my group from Pascoe, Tony Readhead, got a mud ball in the eye and ended up losing permanently the sight in that eye. I am still in good contact with Tony to this day and he has had a quite brilliant career and is a noted professor of Astronomy. Also, during my time at the school we had three boys bitten by puff adder snakes during our Sunday exploits, not a pleasant experience. I hate snakes.

Once, during your time at Michaelhouse, you were expected to go and climb a very large hill called Inhlazane (pronounced inch-la-zaan), a Zulu word which I was always told meant 'woman's breast'. Certainly, the hill bore a considerable resemblance. Folklore decreed that you were not considered to be qualified to be an old boy of the school until you had climbed what was effectively a small mountain, and it was a good challenge. It involved a round trip of walking some 36 miles, including the climb and descent, and you had to set off at between three and four in the morning in order to get back in time for evening chapel. I did this challenge during my third year and it was a great experience, and very satisfying to have successfully completed the task. Our experiences from time spent in the countryside on Sundays taught us much. In the words of one of the school's memorable school phrases, 'Explore, Educate, Excel'.

I have many other memories of my time at Michaelhouse and undoubtedly the most painful one was being beaten with a cane by both masters and prefects. I was beaten on a number of occasions. If it was a beating from a master it would take place in his study and if it was from a prefect then you were normally summoned in your pyjamas after lights out. The maximum number of strokes that I personally received was four and usually three but it made no difference, it always hurt and I was left with the stripes on my bottom, war wounds, which would last for weeks, going blue, grey, yellow, it seemed like every colour in the rainbow. I am very pleased to see that such practice has long since disappeared because I was never convinced that it was an effective punishment, just bloody painful.

Living in Johannesburg, we used to travel to and from school at the beginning and end of each term on a special school train (diesel to a mid-point town, Volksrust, and then we switched to steam) together with boys from our rival boys school, Hilton College, and what we used to regard as our sister girls school, St Anne's. My brothers, both at Cordwalles for my first two years, after which John joined me at Michaelhouse, also travelled on the train. These were always interesting journeys and rather unsupervised. There was one particular train journey from Johannesburg at the start of term in my final year when matters got somewhat out of hand and which resulted in the expulsion of 12 boys. It even hit the newspaper headlines in the UK press with headlines like '12 boys expelled from Eton of South Africa'. I hasten to add that at that stage I was a very clean-living boy and was not involved in any way, thank goodness.

As well as studying for my matriculation exams, which were the university entrance examinations, and all the sport that we played, I also used to do carpentry lessons where I discovered, for the first but not the last time, that I am not the best DIY expert in town. Most things that I made did not fit and when I decided to build a kayak the finished product was useless because the keel was crooked and there was no way that the boat could be rowed in a straight line. Oh well, one lives and learns, one hopes! But I was good at art, which I loved, and I won the art prize in my final two years at Michaelhouse. I also won a prize for English speaking.

Probably my most least celebrated occasion at Michaelhouse was when someone poured liquid over my hair and then told me that it was peroxide and that my hair would change colour within a couple of days. I was then told that I could reverse the process if I washed my hair in Worcester sauce. Gullible as ever, that is exactly what I did and all of a sudden, in the middle of washing my hair in the changing room with said antidote the doors suddenly opened with shrieks of laughter and I was left in no doubt that I had been 'had'. What an idiot but all part of life's rich learning pattern and even I could see the funny side of it all.

There is so much that I could write about Michaelhouse, what a great school, but I can't close this chapter without mentioning a few names of school chums who became special friends. Mike 'Fuzzy' Fergusson was a best friend and, in particular, after we left school. His father was president of the Johannesburg Stock Exchange and he had also been South African motor racing champion. Fuzzy and I used to help out in the commentary box at the Kyalami Race Track near Johannesburg where I met all the famous race drivers of the time, Jim Clark, Graham Hill, Innes Ireland to name but a few. Fuzzy sadly passed away quite a few years ago. Then there is Adrian Leighton-Morris who has been almost a lifelong friend now. I have always valued his friendship and loyalty and we remain in close contact to this day. Michael Sommerlatte was another good friend at school. Of German extraction, he was a super chap but I have long lost contact. I would love to have the opportunity to meet him again. I have happy memories of holidays with his family in game reserves. Clive Macewan was the school squash champion for all four years of his time at Michaelhouse and he went on to be a junior Springbok squash player. He is also, as far as I am aware, the only squash player at the school to have been awarded his honours blazer for his achievements. He lives in London and we regularly meet at the RAF Club where we are both members. Clive is a first-class chap and a good friend. Then there is John Rae who was a bit of a wild young man, as I was, in our early years as Michaelhouse Old Boys. And there are so many others that I would like to mention and haven't, some no longer with us, regrettably, but all of whom have a special place in my memories. One thing though is fact and that is that a very large majority of boys who were schooled at Michaelhouse have gone on to become leaders and big achievers in every walk of life. It is a school that trains boys well for their future roles in life. I for one owe the school a debt for what the education I received has given to me and I remain in close contact with the school and the old boys club. I sit on the UK committee where I am known as the 'Elder Statesman'. I have also, twice now, spoken to the whole school in the Schlesinger theatre auditorium at the school, occasions that have given me considerable pleasure and pride. I am very proud indeed to call myself a Michaelhouse old boy. 'Quis Ut Deus' (the school motto).

I must also say a few words about the many holidays that we had with our parents in the school breaks. We often went to the Kruger National Park to view the game, always a great experience. I remember, in particular, the day that a rogue bull elephant, that my father was filming crossing the road, suddenly stopped in the middle of the road, his large ears opened wide and flapped and he charged our car. My father had much of the experience on film until he quickly put the car in reverse and as soon as the car started to move the elephant veered off into the bush. Our heart rates were certainly raised by this experience. We had many holidays on the south coast of Natal, usually at a lovely seaside resort called Southbroom. We had a holiday in the Drakensberg Mountains and other weekends in the lush green eastern Transvaal at a place called Magoebaskloof and at Hartebeestpoort Dam not too far from Johannesburg.

Also, my brother John and I, when I was 13 and he was 12, went by ourselves to northern Rhodesia to stay with my Aunt Judy and her family at their home in a place called Wankie. Her husband, John, was the district commissioner for the area at that time. I especially remember this holiday for a number of reasons. It was a very long train journey each way; whilst in Wankie I experienced my first kiss; John ended up in a spot of trouble when he rolled a rock off the top of a hill which crashed through a wooden hut at the bottom of the hill; we were both in trouble, me because I was the older and had not prevented the incident. Finally, we nearly hit an elephant in the Wankie Game Reserve. We had visited the game reserve in the afternoon and were leaving in the dark after having had evening drinks with the head warden. Very exciting!

I should also add that it was not long after our return to South Africa that my parents bought another house, 18 Arran Avenue in Illovo, only a quarter of a mile from the magnificent sporting facilities at the Wanderers Club where we became members. In the holidays we played tennis and squash but most of our time was spent at the Wanderers Golf Club where John and I learnt to play golf. I used to play golf almost every day in the school holidays and I quickly got down to a handicap of 16. I also remember one day, at the age of just 15, I actually completed nine holes with a par score of 36. I was so keen on golf that I used to get up at five o'clock in the morning and cycle to the golf club to look for golf balls before returning for my breakfast. These were good days.

I left Michaelhouse with a 2nd Class Matric in December 1961, all that I needed to go on to university. I was always a year younger than others in my class and matriculated at age 16 for entry to the University of Witwatersrand (Wits) in Johannesburg. I really wanted to go to Cape Town University but my parents, especially my mother, were insistent that I lived at home while at the university, as I had spent so many years away from home as a boarder (probably not the right decision at the time but I took full advantage of it).

I went to Wits not knowing what I really wanted to study, after all I was still only 16. However, I had won the art prize at school for the previous couple of years and was therefore interested in a possible career as an architect or in industrial design. My aptitude tests had also shown that I had great potential in a career associated with both art and mathematics. I decided against architecture by reason that it would have taken seven years of study and what I really wanted to do was three years at university and then go out into the big wide world. Therefore, I entered university to study for a BA (Fine Arts) degree (definitely, another wrong decision in my life).

I started my university course and enjoyed the practical side of art. However, the other courses in my first year, namely Classical Life and Thought, History and History of Art were, apart from History of Art, not my cup of tea. I do remember arriving late for my first class associated with 'Drawing from Life', when I opened the door to be confronted by a nude lady. I thought that drawing from life was all about leaves and plants, but the class became the one class that I never missed!

At the conclusion of my first year at university I failed all my subjects apart from the one subject in which I had had a real interest, namely Theory and Practice of Art. I had basically had too good a time in my first year. I felt that it was really only at university that I was beginning to mature, although my children would still question that now when I am in my 70s. I also discovered wine, women and song and had too good a time, it was as if I had finally found freedom after being let out of a cage and I went fairly wild, some would say very wild! My father said that he was reluctant to pay for another year as a full-time student at Wits but I wanted to get a degree and so I decided to try a different route. At that time, a career in flying was beginning to dominate my thoughts but I did not think that I would be eligible to join the RAF. Instead, I set out to become a chartered accountant and I became an articled clerk to a firm of accountants in Johannesburg, Alex Aitken and Carter. I went to university in the early morning, worked as an articled clerk during the day and then returned to university for more studies in the early evening. I also attended lectures on Saturday mornings. I was studying for a CA qualification. With my strong aptitude for mathematics I very much enjoyed this second year at Wits and I passed my exams.

As well as enjoying my time at university, my life away from the university was quite outstanding. Whilst there were many friends from my time at Michaelhouse I met many other people in Jo'burg and we all led a very, very active social life, and that is putting it mildly. I was living a life of luxury at home and I was getting to know lots of girls, most of whom were in their final year at Roedean School including the girl who, for most of the time, was my main girlfriend, Liz Swan. She was an absolutely lovely girl but, for a lot of the time that we were dating, I just was not ready to go 'steady' with one girl. Girls from Kingsmead and St Mary's were also very much involved with the emerging party set. My parents had bought me a 70cc Itom Super Sport 'Buzz Bike' and I used to enjoy riding this to and from university and to wherever the next party took place. I got my driving licence at the first attempt when I was just 17 and my mother used to very kindly lend me her Morris Minor, far too often! I must have been a great worry to my parents during this period because I drove like a cowboy and I regret to say that I had more than one or two scrapes in my mother's car. I am not proud of this achievement. As my good friend, Adrian Leighton-Morris wrote recently:

'I have known Rick since we were at school together at Michaelhouse. We have been friends for over 60 years. In the times between Michael-house and Rick joining the RAF and while at university he was a "very wild young man" in the wine, women and song society set of Johannesburg.

'He is one of the few men I know who took out both twin sisters [I would dispute this, I only took out one at a time!] and they never seemed to mind…visiting the said twins one night he woke up their father. He did a fast exit in his mother's Morris Minor, but collided with the family tree in the driveway. I remember he called on all his friends to help draft the letter to the father explaining a) how he managed to drive into the tree "cold sober" and b) what he was doing in the driveway in the first place?

'I do believe he once managed to roll a go-kart on the track at the Blue Lagoon in Durban. A further example of his remarkable driving skills… I also recall going to the holiday resort of Plettenberg Bay, lying in South Africa's Garden Route, with Rick and his brother John in the Morris saloon. We covered 2,500 miles and used 50 pints of oil (only exceeded by the quantity of beer consumed).

'I can still picture him one Sunday evening. His parents had moved to a house near William Nicol Drive in Johannesburg and Rick invited some friends around to his home for a Sunday evening braai. He appeared at the top of the stairs in his father's full Royal Air Force uniform and told us he was off to join the RAF– it was the first I had ever heard of that plan.

'I am afraid that none of these recollections help to explain the great career heights he achieved but maybe that was in an era after he had left us behind!'

In early 1964, in what would have been my third year at university, I had a fairly major appendix operation (it had been rumbling for some time). I lost three months of studies following surgery and began to think even more if I really wanted to become an accountant, or did I want to fly. The answer, of course, was a no brainer and that was the point at which I definitely decided that I wanted to fly and voluntarily left university.

At this stage I had done more than two years at Wits University when I applied to join the RAF. However, there was no guarantee that I would be accepted for pilot training and so, testing the waters, I also applied for a management trainee job with Lever Brothers in Durban, which required a degree (which I didn't have). Yet I was offered the job and went to live in Durban, taking up the post of a management trainee, which I found very interesting.

Whilst starting the job with Lever Brothers I was also going through various procedures to join the RAF including an aptitude test at Wits University which again highlighted my mathematical instincts. I took my medical tests with the South African Air Force and then had my final interview at the British Defence Liaison Staff headquarters in Pretoria. The headquarters was a lovely place and situated in the leafy suburbs, more appropriate to socialising than for business. My final interview for suitability for pilot training was conducted by the head of the headquarters, Air Commodore Tomalin, who was supported by Wing Commander Speed and a squadron leader from the headquarters.

The interview took place on a Friday and my interviewers were flying off to Basutoland that afternoon, in the aircraft allocated to the headquarters, for a weekend of trout fishing and I remember thinking what a perfect life! Following my interview, waiting in the lounge, they came through to say, "Congratulations Rick, we've accepted you for pilot training; when would you like to sail and what would you like to drink?" I really warmed to this and thought what a perfect way to start my career with the RAF. The interview happened at the end of November 1964 and I thought to myself that I needed a holiday at Plettenberg Bay to say farewell to all of my friends, and so I told them in about six weeks. Oh, and I, of course, accepted the drink! I almost forgot that I had to tell Lever Brothers what I was doing but they were very good and fully understood, thank goodness. I never looked back, the best decision of my life. I should add that my girlfriend, Liz Swan (we are still in good contact), had sat patiently outside in my mother's famous car, which I had borrowed as usual, whilst I was enjoying my first pint of beer with the RAF.

Having decided to join the RAF I remember one particular effort to try and change my mind. The father of one of my really good friends in Johannesburg invited me to meet him at his house one Sunday morning. He was the managing director of a very large and important company. Over morning coffee he said to me: "Rick, I hear you are going to join the RAF?" To which I replied affirmatively. He responded to this with: "You are making a big mistake. You have a greater opportunity if you remain in business in South Africa. Come and work for me and I will give you a starting salary of 'x' amount." 'X' being a very large and attractive sum of money. However I declined his kind offer and have never looked back.

Six weeks later, I set sail on the *Cape Town Castle*, a Union Castle passenger liner to the UK to begin my RAF training. This was a fantastic experience and involved two weeks at sea from Cape Town to Southampton via Madeira. There were two other South Africans travelling with me for the same purpose, Tony Cook, a St John's Old Boy and Grant Whitten who had attended Pretoria Grammar School. We had fun and, certainly for me, it was definitely a 'wine, women and song' trip. It was also quite an eventful trip. Winston Churchill died whilst we were at sea, I celebrated my 20th birthday, and a gold bullion robbery on board had been discovered during the voyage. When we arrived at Southampton on a grey February morning in 1965 my first recollection of the UK was that I could not understand a word that the dockers were saying, they sounded like foreigners to my ears.

I had now arrived in the UK ready to begin what felt to me was both another step into the unknown but also the next phase of the adventure of life. I once again felt like an outsider and I did not really know what to expect. I was just 20 years old and, even though I had previously lived in England for a number of years, I was back on the other side of the world from the rest of my family. Once again, I suddenly had feelings of doubt and wondered if I made the right decision.

CHAPTER 3
LIFE IN THE
RAF BEGINS

To clarify right up front a question that I am often asked, namely, why I had joined the RAF and not the South African Air Force. The reasons are various but there are four main ones. First, my father had been in the RAF and was a Battle of Britain pilot and I wanted to follow in his footsteps. Second, the RAF was, and still is, in my view, the very best air force in the world, and, importantly from a historical perspective, was also the world's first independent air force. Third, I knew that I would be unlikely to be selected to fly a high-performance fighter, the Mirage in South Africa, until I was well into my 30s and I also knew that I could become a Lightning pilot, my dream aircraft, and as I did, straight from training. And finally, I always regarded, possibly wrongly so, that the South African Air Force was more dominated by the Afrikaans language and I was English. I was totally focused on the RAF.

The start of my journey to become a fighter pilot really goes back to before I went through the selection process in South Africa when I was beginning to think seriously of following in my father's footsteps. I obtained a brochure about becoming a pilot in the RAF and on the front cover were the words 'Join the Royal Air Force and the World is your Oyster'. Well, that certainly caught my attention but what caught my attention even more was the photo on the front cover. It was of a squadron of Lightnings, No. 74 Squadron, lined up on the aircraft servicing platform with a group of pilots walking back to the squadron from the aircraft, who had obviously just returned from a mission. I pointed at that photo and I said there and then, "That is me". I never looked back from that moment or those words, my mind was made up.

After arrival at Southampton there was enough time to sample the delights of London over a weekend with my fellow traveller and new RAF recruit, Tony Cook, before reporting to RAF South Cerney, near Cirencester in Gloucestershire for officer training. At South Cerney I joined No. 209 Officer Training Course in February 1965. Back in South Africa I had been told that they would have sent me to the RAF College at Cranwell but for my age. I was 20 and the age limit to enter Cranwell was 19-and-a-half. My officer training lasted from February until May 1965 and was intense. It was a very good test in every way, it was demanding, as it should be, and I got very fit and learned a lot. I enjoyed the challenge and the desire to graduate as an officer was strong, which drove me to put everything into my training and to strive to achieve the best results. However, and most importantly, having had it instilled in my brain in South Africa that South Africans were the best, I was very pleasantly surprised to discover that my fellow British officer cadet trainees were a very able bunch of people and, individually and collectively, every bit as good or even better than their South African counterparts. The people that I have met in the RAF over the years have never changed that opinion.

The first few days at South Cerney were definitely a shock to the system. We had a haircut on day one, were kitted out with uniforms, sports kit and more and seemed to be on the drill square and in the gym in no time at all. Indoctrination into the RAF was sudden and quick. We also sat initial exams in mathematics, English and science, presumably to give an insight into our knowledge. Whatever, it was a good move because, whist I flourished with the mathematics and English that was not the case with science which I had given up studying two years before I matriculated in South Africa. I achieved a very low mark in science and I knew that I had a lot of hard work ahead of me in order to reach the required standard for graduation. We were introduced to the civilian tailors because we were expected to adhere to certain dress standards; on our infrequent days off base we had to wear sports jacket and tie and a trilby hat was a compulsory feature, after all we were being trained to become officers!

There were many facets to officer training, designed not only to train you to the required standard in many different ways but also to confirm that you had what it took to be an officer. There were a number of trainees, we were known as officer cadets, who failed at various stages and returned to civvy street, others needed more time and training and were re-coursed. The most challenging part of the course revolved around leadership training and it was in this area that I probably learnt most about myself. I found that I thrived on a challenge and used to very much enjoy being thrust into any leadership role. We used to complete exercises on the nearby lakes, fondly remembered as the gravel pits, and they were mentally demanding exercises, and the biggest test came when we went on a one-week camp in the Brecon Beacons in Wales. This was really the final maker or breaker of the course to demonstrate your potential as an officer. It was also where I quickly found that I definitely seemed to have a flair for leadership. I particularly remember one very demanding night-time exercise where we had to walk and navigate our way over quite a distance to make a rendezvous in the morning; it was a test of both mental and physical strength and fitness. As I recall, I was in a team of six and not the initially appointed leader, we were allocated responsibilities and it was quite clear that the directing staff were watching for confirmation or otherwise of our strengths and weaknesses. On this particular night, as the exercise progressed and the challenges increased I found myself naturally thrust towards a leadership role as others floundered around me, I think because they were having to concentrate on the physical side but at the expense of being able to cope with the mental test associated with leadership. It taught me a lot about myself and it also taught me about the strengths and weaknesses of others, an issue that I was again to experience on a survival course some years later. I learnt that I could lead, that I was not a quitter, that I had a strong stamina; I learnt about ME. It gave me great confidence in my own abilities. Talking about that particular night, I will never forget us arriving at the rendezvous point feeling very tired and even more hungry. There was a very strong smell of breakfast being cooked and, as I write these words, I can still smell those sausages and bacon etc. being cooked. However, we were nowhere near being able to have a good meal, we had another eight hours of walking to reach our allocated camp site and then we had to use our parachutes to make shelters.

I progressively enjoyed my time in officer training more and more, partly because, as the course progressed, we were becoming increasingly integrated with the officer fraternity, and partly because spring had arrived and it was delightful weather. Amongst our instructional staff and the station hierarchy there were plenty of those who were veterans of World War II and some had a very impressive array of medals. They had all been involved with the RAF front line and therefore had considerable experience. I was in awe.

Those on my course were from a mixed array of backgrounds and the youngest of which had already completed two weeks at an outward-bound school before commencing officer training. The accents were various, from posh English to strong South African. There was even a young Liverpudlian who had had to have some elocution training to make his accent better under-stood. If he reads these words then he will know exactly who I am talking about, and he went on to have a very successful career in the RAF. The youngest was 17 and the oldest in his late 20s and with a Cambridge degree in his locker. But the most impressive thing that I remember was the cama-raderie that quickly developed on the course, camaraderie that I was to experience throughout my RAF career, an irreplaceable strength within all the British armed forces.

For the first month of training we lived in a barrack block where I still recall with a smile on my face the chap in the next bed to mine, Al Robinson was his name, regularly saying to me in his London accent, "Get off my f***ing bed space". The 'bed spaces', for which we were individually responsible were inspected every day. We were certainly being instilled with discipline. We then moved to the number two officers' mess for the second and third months of training, single rooms in a wooden hut, before spending the final month in the main officers' mess, a very imposing building built very much along the lines of so many other large wartime officers' messes. And whilst living there, we were granted full privileges, as I recall, which I also greatly appreciated. I remember, in that final month, I really felt that I was getting the best insight into life in the officers' mess, my future home, and those who were already in that privileged position – it certainly excited my interest for the future.

At the end of May we had our graduation parade and graduated as acting pilot officers, a very momentous day and one that I will never forget. I was only sad that my parents, or for that matter any members of my close family, were not able to be present for what was one of the proudest days of my life. I then had three weeks' holiday before commencing my next phase of development, basic flying training. I spent the time with my grandmother in Jersey. Mind you, without a home to go to in the UK and no money – I had been paid the substantial sum of eight pounds per week during officer training – there were nights during my travels when I slept on a chair at Heathrow and on a bench at Waterloo, always discreetly and in disguise, because I could not afford anything more luxurious. Happy memories, and I mean that seriously because to me it was all part of life's rich pattern, it taught me a lot, and I never take anything for granted.

On completion of my officer training I was posted to No. 6 Flying Training School, RAF Acklington, on the coast of Northumberland in the north-east of England. I looked at a map to see where Acklington was and my initial thought was goodness, it is on the other side of the world! Well, all I can say is that I had the most fantastic year in Northumberland, a very beautiful and welcoming county. I have nothing but happy memories of the experience, from the flying, my fellow course members, the local people, the scenery, the golf, the parties, everything.

There were 27 members on my basic flying training course, some of whom I had met on my officer training course, others came from within the RAF or from other officer training courses at South Cerney. There were five members of the course who were older than most, three of whom had been air electronics operators (AEOs) on the Valiant fleet of aircraft which had been grounded due to a wing spar failure. Their names were Mike Barnes, who became a lifelong friend and retired as an air commodore, and who, I believe, might have even been a member of the crew of the aircraft which led to the permanent grounding of the Valiant fleet. The others, as I recall, were Dave Hodgkinson and Pete Harris, who were all already flight lieutenants whilst most of us were acting pilot officers, and they were, in our eyes, very senior and experienced. The other two older course members were Steve Stevenson, who wore the brevet of an air signaller and Ed Viney, who had been an engineering technician in the RAF. They were all very important members of my course – father figures you might say.

There were so many characters, I could talk about them all but the ones who I especially remember are Jim Uprichard, from Northern Ireland, and who had spent time at Queen's University. He already held the rank of pilot officer because of his previous experience, he played the guitar, told good stories, drank beer and played rugby to a very high standard. He went on to have a very successful RAF career and retired as an air commodore. Like Mike Barnes, he became a lifelong friend and we see a lot of each other, we live in the same area and we meet for dinner, with our wives, every few months. Bob Eccles was a Scotsman and another lively person. He too went on to have a distinguished flying career. He flew Harriers and was a member of the Red Arrows aerobatic team before moving into commercial aviation where he was a captain with easyJet. Very sadly, he died of a brain tumour far too young but not before Jim Uprichard and I had flown up to Prestwick to see him in his final days. I will always remember the lunch that we had with Bob during this visit, plus an afternoon of reminiscing. The bond was as strong as ever and both Jim and I agreed that it had been a very special experience and one that neither of us will ever forget. The fortitude and resolve of Bob were nothing but inspirational. Dai James was another character who liked a good party, he was also an excellent pilot and a good sportsman. We were both to fly Lightnings and some years later I was best man at his wedding. Bill Campbell was another Scotsman who already had a good experience of life. He too played a good game of rugby even if his rugby kit never saw the laundry. Bill Lee was from the Midlands in England and another lively character who, like most on the course, had a prang or two in his car, in his case a Sunbeam Alpine. And then there was my fellow journeyman from South Africa, Tony Cook. All I can say about Tony is that he was a unique character, very difficult to sum up and sometimes difficult to understand. He was his own man but very supportive, and a man who always gave maximum effort. I lost contact with Tony after the end of basic flying training when our future lives went in different directions but I would love to meet him again and fill in the gaps. I am told that he hides somewhere in Lincolnshire.

It was a great course, a first-class bunch of chaps, and we quickly bonded into a group with plenty of course spirit (some would say coarse!). The camaraderie was excellent, and so were the parties. What a year we had at RAF Acklington and in Northumberland.

Our basic flying training course itself was to last one year. There was a lot to learn both in the air (general handling including aerobatics, instrument flying, medium- and low-level navigation, formation flying, night flying) and on the ground (subjects included technical, engines, aerodynamics, principles of flight, meteorology, aviation medicine, aviation law, navigation, airmanship, combat survival and history of the RAF). To succeed, as in all walks of life, you had to work hard but I have always been ambitious and enjoyed the hard work ethic. In my view, the effort that I put in in those early days, essentially to establish a platform for the future, stood me in good stead throughout my RAF career. Unlike many others, I had not completed a piston-engine Chipmunk course before commencing flying training on the Jet Provost. I was, therefore, to become what is known as a 'straight through jet jockey'. I flew solo for the first time in 1965, at RAF Ouston, after about 12 hours flying training. My instructor, Kit Pitcher, had been a co-pilot on Shackletons before becoming a flying instructor.

I can remember well, to this day, all of the flying on the course. We first had a familiarisation sortie, a freebie to 'whet the appetite', and that it did. There I was in a Jet Provost, all kitted out in what to me at the time was space-age clothing, and about to launch myself into the unknown. Could I predict the future? The answer was no, I most certainly could not, but all I knew was that I have never wanted to succeed more in all my life. In particular, to atone to my parents for what I had considered a rather immature few years at university, and I wanted to prove to my father that, like him, I had the ability to fly. I have never been so determined. As we accelerated down the runway on that first sortie I remember my thoughts: thrilling; I love the speed; how am I going to meet my aspirations; this is going to be a challenge; I will not be beaten. I found the pre-solo phase particularly tough, mainly because it was all so new. I worked hard and I have never felt so much elation as when I went solo for the first time. I cannot fully describe the thrill, or the feeling of responsibility, to be airborne by myself, it was to me the greatest achievement in my life thus far, but I also had to land. I remember there was a crosswind on my first solo sortie and that worried me slightly without my instructor there to offer guidance or tell me when and where I was going wrong. However, the fact that I am writing these words today means that I safely arrived back on terra firma, even if, as the aircraft was crabbing into wind on the final approach, I couldn't help feeling that I was aiming at the runway caravan. Nevertheless, this day, the 9th of September 1965, remains one of the most memorable days of my life. It felt like a launching point into my flying career.

We progressed through the course, from flying phase to flying phase, the flying interspersed with our ground studies during the first half of the course. There were a number of hurdles to jump in our flying, going solo was the first but then came a number of instrument flying tests culminating in an instrument rating test, a basic handling test, a night-flying test, a final navigation test and, finally, a final handling test which we had to pass before graduation and the award of the coveted RAF Wings. My confidence and ability grew as the course progressed and I can well remember my lightbulb moment which came during the instrument flying phase of the course. To this day I find it hard to explain but I found that, as I undertook instrument flying – which included learning how to recover on instruments from unusual positions – these could have been from almost any situation – going vertically up or down – or upside down with nothing on the clock (no speed) – it was like a green light was lit. All of a sudden, I seemed to understand much better what I was trying to do flying an aircraft. Quite simply, I never looked back from that moment onwards, which must have been at about the 30-40 hours of flying point on the course, and flying, to me, since that moment, has always felt 100 per cent natural. I just loved all of my time in the air, and don't get me wrong, it was all still a challenge because, as each new flying phase of the course arrived, there was more to learn. However, by the end of the course I not only came near to the top of the flying element of the course but I had been entered into the competition for the aerobatics trophy and I won the navigation trophy. I flew with Flying Officer Kit Pitcher, for the first half of the course, until we changed squadrons, and then I flew with my second instructor, Flight Lieutenant Roger Smith, a fairly new teacher who had previously flown the Canberra. A big chap, and another fine rugby player as I recall, I also remember thinking to myself towards the end of my basic flying training that I was able to fly the Jet Provost every bit as well as he could. That was a mark of how far I had come, and a growing awareness of my ability, although I was *never* complacent.

My particular flying course was also notable because the failure rate was very low, only two or three as I recall and we also had no flying accidents on the course. You might wonder why I say this but, in those days, the flying accident rate was still very high by modern-day standards and it was rare for there to be none at all.

RAF Acklington was a place that most people loved and there was an excellent bunch of high-quality aviators who were the instructors, many with a lot of front-line operational experience and many who went on to greater things in their RAF careers. Names that come to mind are John Willis, Richie Profit, Tim Webb, John Houghton, Ken Clark, Al Cleaver, Dave Mulinder, Tom Stonor, Colin Adams, and there were many more. The chief instructor, a wing commander, was a South African named Swart. His presence alone, he was a nice friendly man with a very fine RAF moustache, made me feel at home. I liked all of the instructors and I remember them well. It was another new phase of my life and, as throughout my initial years in the RAF, I was in awe of their flying achievements, and envious that they already knew so much. I was hungry to learn.

The ground school I found much more difficult than the airborne side and I certainly had to work hard. My exam results were very average but I passed and, more importantly, I had learnt a tremendous amount which was to serve me well in the future. The ground school instructors were also mainly very experienced RAF aircrew and they knew their subjects. The chief ground instructor, Squadron Leader Roly Jackson was a well-known Lightning pilot who would reappear in my life some years later when I was flying Lightnings and he returned to the fighter world.

On the work side, one thing that I remember is the survival exercise conducted in remote parts of Northumberland. We would simulate having had to eject in such an environment. We were dropped at a location, simulating where we had landed in our parachutes, and then had to navigate our way, over some distance, and by night and day, to reach a number of rendezvous points. We had to survive for several days with just the equipment that we would have had with us in the aircraft, namely a parachute from our ejection and a dinghy pack from the ejection seat, plus what we might have in our own flying clothing, such things as maps and knives. We would be wearing cold-weather clothing and this was very helpful. We learnt how to navigate over tricky terrain and by night and day, and also how to use our parachutes as a tent, and our dinghies as a mattress. The contents of our dinghy packs included such things as enough specially compacted food to keep you alive for a few days, matches, a fishing line, water-making kit, and flares. It was an incredibly useful and very practical few days and we all learnt a lot even if it was putting into practice what we had been taught in the classroom. Most importantly, we learnt about ourselves as well as learning the art of combat survival.

And there was much more, such as dinghy drills; that is learning how to use our dinghy if one ever had to eject into water, in both the swimming pool and at sea where we would also be winched up from the sea and into a search and rescue helicopter. There was also drill on the parade square because we still needed to retain the ability to march and take part in military parades, not least our own graduation parade. We did physical training in the gym and the opportunities for sport were great. As everywhere that I have been in the RAF, the sporting facilities were excellent and we took full advantage of our good fortune. Overall, the curriculum was full and it was both rewarding and satisfying.

Returning now to the social side of my time in Northumberland, I, quite simply, had a great time. Away from the officers' mess our social life seemed to be mainly, but not completely, focused on a teachers' training college in a local town, Alnwick. A number of girls from the college lived in a large rambling house in Alnwick called Ravenslaw, the scene of many a party. A number of my fellow students ended up marrying girls from Ravenslaw. At the time I was still trying to stay in touch, from afar, with my girlfriend in South Africa, Liz Swan, who was by now at Natal University in Pietermaritzburg. We used to write to each other a lot but I don't pretend that it was not becoming increasingly difficult, for both of us, to stay closely in touch, and I certainly found that I needed female company. As well as the girls from Alnwick I also started to go out with a girl from Newcastle, a lovely lass called Christine Smart. We only remained in contact whilst I was at Acklington and she herself was about to start a career in the Foreign Office. I have no idea in which direction life took her but I remember her well. At the time, I drove an old Morris Oxford, it must have cost me about £30 but it served its purpose well, that was until I fell asleep at the wheel returning from a party in Newcastle at about six a.m. one Sunday morning and ended up in a ditch. My passenger, a large fellow student from Acklington called Taff Hinchcliff (he later flew Lightnings and Jaguars but, unfortunately, died in a flying accident some years later) fell on top of me as the car was on its side and I think that was how one of the bones in my shoulder became detached at a joint. I was very depressed, not because I had written off my car but because I was now going to be off flying and I could see a re-course on the horizon and that was the last thing that I wanted to happen. Fortunately, I was very fit, recovered quicker than expected and was back in the air after just two weeks when I had actually been told by the doctors that the healing could take up to six weeks. My depression turned into elation.

Towards the end of the course, those charged with deciding in which direction our future flying would be concentrated, i.e. the future direction of our flying careers, told me that they were keen to send me to helicopters where they needed people with good leadership potential. I was not interested; all I wanted to be was a fighter pilot. A week later my squadron commander again told me that they wanted to send me to helicopters and I declined again. Fortunately, as far as I was concerned, I came near to the top of the course and I got what I wanted and was posted to RAF Valley, on the island of Anglesey, to complete my advanced flying training on the Folland Gnat. I was on my way to becoming a fighter pilot. One final comment about the possibility of being streamed to helicopters, I would like to put it on record that I have always had the greatest of respect for helicopter pilots and I had the privilege of learning to fly helicopters myself in the latter days of my RAF career, it was just that I dearly wanted to be a fighter pilot.

My 'Wings' graduation took place at RAF Acklington on 24th June 1966. I remember the graduating officer who presented me with them was Field Marshal Sir Francis Festing, a very impressive-looking army officer who was fully booted and spurred for the occasion in ceremonial uniform. It was the proudest day of my life thus far. I was just sorry that once again no one from my family could be there to celebrate the occasion with me but I fully understood and in those days travel to and from South Africa was not as easy as it is today. However, photographs did appear in the South African press. Of interest, I didn't even speak to my parents on the phone for my first two years away from home. Telephone communication was difficult and we mainly stayed in touch by air mail letter and, if urgent, by telegram. How times have changed!

As well as the regular contact that I have had with Mike Barnes and Jim Uprichard over the 53 plus years since our graduation, I have also seen many of the others but there are also a number of my fellow course members whom I have not seen, some since our graduation. If any of them happen to read these words then I would love them to make contact. We did have a memorable reunion, at the RAF Club in London, in June 2016, to celebrate the 50th anniversary of our graduation. On that very special occasion, it was quite apparent that there remained a very strong bond between all of us who were present.

Now it was off to the next phase of my training adventure, advanced flying training, with wings proudly displayed on my uniform. I had difficulty taking my eyes off them.

Following my graduation I remained at Acklington for a short while before commencing my advanced flying training in August at RAF Valley. I immediately liked Valley, the base was situated right by the sea and the views of the Snowdonia mountain range were panoramic. The beaches were sandy and the officers' mess overlooked a lake. It was a very active base and it was great to see so many aircraft flying, mainly Folland Gnats. However, it was especially good to also see Lightnings flying from Valley. Lightning squadrons were detached to the Strike Command Air-to-Air Missile Establishment located on the far side of the airfield and from where aircraft carried out sorties to fire missiles in a range in Cardigan Bay off the Welsh coast. Valley was also a master emergency diversion airfield, or MEDA as it was known, and was open 24 hours a day. During the winter months we saw a number of aircraft which had been diverted to Valley, usually because of fog or snow at their parent bases. This included a number of Vulcans, always an impressive sight on take-off. We really felt that we were getting closer to the front line, and our ultimate aim of becoming operational pilots.

The aircraft on which we did our advanced flying training was the Gnat. A small aircraft, it could go supersonic in a dive, it was highly manoeuvrable and had a very fast rate of roll. The Gnat was a quantum leap forward from the Jet Provost and I loved flying the aircraft, it was like a sports car. The aircraft itself was demanding, the swept-wing characteristics were different from those of a 'straight wing' and, importantly, everything happened faster and therefore you had to think and react quicker. This environment seemed to suit me well and I loved the flying.

On our course, we first had to learn about the Gnat in ground school and, for the first time in our short flying careers, there was also a simulator to assist with training. We were trained in the simulator to fly the aircraft, manage the systems and practise emergencies. It was a very useful training aid in which to prepare us for the actual flying. By the time we started the flying phase of our course we had to know well the cockpit checks and aircraft limitations, and how to cope with emergencies. The Gnat had been brought into service specifically to prepare trainee pilots for aircraft such as the Lightning. To this end, the instrumentation was basically the same as in the Lightning and we were introduced to systems and procedures that would be compatible with that aircraft. The Gnat moved around the sky at speed and could go much higher than the Jet Provost. On recovery to Valley, at the end of a sortie, we would recover through a dive arc. We learned how to use the tactical air navigation system, known as TACAN. This was a very useful aid and especially so because there was an offset capability. This enabled us to choose other offset points away from the transmitting beacon to where we could accurately navigate and fly. That is what we did when recovering to Valley through the dive arc when we would descend to an offset point, known as Point Alpha. This was at a range from Valley which then enabled us either to enter the radar pattern, if recovering in bad weather, or to position the Gnat to do a visual join into the circuit.

A good knowledge of emergency drills was essential not just because you had to be able to react quickly but also because there were some emergency drills which, if you got the drills wrong, could kill you, in particular the drill for a hydraulic system failure where you had to revert to a secondary control of the aircraft tailplane. I can still remember the mnemonic for the drill, as follows:

S – Speed
T – Trim to six degrees nose-up
U – Unlock the elevators
P – Power off
R – Raise the guard
E – Exhaust the accumulators
C – Check the trim
C – Check the controls

If you didn't set the trim correctly you could run out of control of the aircraft. There were other gotchas as well but one of the most important things to learn about were the swept-wing flying characteristics and in particular, the stalling traits. A lack of knowledge or understanding in this area could also cause you harm. The other interesting characteristic on the Gnat was the fact that the aircraft had what are known as dihedral wings. Landings in a cross-wind could be interesting, partly because of the effect of the airflow over the wings and partly because of the braking system. This was especially so on a wet runway. The Gnat is the only aircraft that I have flown where it can feel on occasions that you were having to fly the aircraft on the ground as well as in the air.

The course itself covered much of the same type of syllabus as at basic flying school: general handling, instrument flying, night flying, high- and low-level navigation and formation flying but, as I have already said, flying in an aircraft with a greater capability, and more advanced avionics, than the Jet Provost. And, of course, an important part of the course was learning about swept-wing flying characteristics and high-speed flight in the transonic region.

Our flying was mainly conducted between ground level and up to 40,000 feet. On take-off the aircraft would accelerate rapidly and we would climb at around 350 knots. Most of our medium-level handling took place between 10,000 and 20,000 feet and included a lot of aerobatics. Low-level flying was particularly exhilarating and flown at speeds up to 420 knots. The aircraft used to move fast and there was a lot to learn about low-level navigation at those speeds. Much of the navigation phase involved high-low-high navigation exercises. We would fly to the other side of the country at high level and then descend down to low level for the low-level phase of the sortie. Then, when we had reached our simulated target we would climb and return to base at high level. These sorties were demanding. Low flying through Wales was a great experience with so many valleys, mountains, lakes, and some very beautiful scenery. We would often have to find a remote target, usually a red telephone box or similar which required pinpoint navigation. There was little room for error and you had to have your wits about you at all times, also there was always fuel and weather to consider. It was all a great challenge and hugely satisfying to achieve success, and success was usually gained through good sortie preparation and accurate flying.

In the higher levels we used to loop the Gnat from 25,000 feet. This exercise was carried out to teach us both the effects of high-speed flight and also the thinner air at high level. We would start the loop from Mach 0.9 and top at about 35,000 feet at a low speed. This demonstrated the effects very well. There was a purpose to all of the flying on the course and we all learned a lot. The Gnat was an ideal aircraft on which to learn and the perfect lead-in trainer to the Lightning.

There were 26 fellow students on my course. Some had been on my basic flying course with me at Acklington, others came from one of the other basic flying training schools, and in the 1960s there were five (Acklington, Syerston, Leeming, Church Fenton and Cranwell). A sizeable element of the course were university graduates who, because of their experience of flying on a university air squadron, had together done a special basic flying training course. Those who were on my course and had come with me from Acklington, as I recall, were Mike Barnes, Dai James, Bob Eccles and Paul Martin. Others had joined an earlier course at Valley. Mike Barnes had become an invaluable friend and he used to help me a lot, particularly with my ground studies where I had to work hard. He had got married in between basic and advanced flying training to a lovely lady called Alison. She had been an air stewardess with Eagle Air. I think I must have been their first house guest, after they had got married, at their new rented home on Anglesey.

My instructor was a very agreeable man called Hugh Maclaughlin, a Scotsman and a university graduate. He had been posted to become an instructor after time in the V-Force. I was his first student and we got on very well. Most of the instructors had come from the operational front line, a number of them from the Lightning or Hunter and others from the Canberra or V-Force. There were three or four who had been specially 'creamed off' straight from training to become instructors. Their introduction to the operational front line would be delayed until after they had completed their instructional tours. They were all a great bunch and I was to fly with a number of the instructors on the front line in later years. Names that come to mind are Ernie Jones, Len Morgan, Peter Dodworth, Bruce Latton, Bob Manning, Dave Baron, Mike Barringer, Pete Chapman, Jerry Lee, Dougie Mee, Bob Turner, Sid Bottom, Mike Vickers, Porky Munro, Anthony Mumford, and there were many more.

The social life was as good as ever and there seemed to be no shortage of girls on the island. We used to frequent the bar in the Treaddur Bay Hotel which was a good meeting place. There were parties in the officers' mess and once a month we would have a dining-in night, dressed in our resplendent new mess kits and wearing the rank of pilot officer in gold braid and with miniature wings on the left lapel of the jacket. It was all still so new and exciting. Dining-in night dinners were usually followed by mess games, some individual and some in teams. They were great fun and would usually lead eventually to a game of mess rugby which was every bit as challenging as it might sound! They were more often than not very late nights which required a long lie-in the following morning.

At the end of the course, in February 1967, we had our course dining-out night in the officers' mess and I was very surprised when my name was announced as the winner of the flying trophy. I knew that I had done reasonably well on the course but I honestly thought that there were others who had done better. I think one of the contributary factors behind that thinking related to what I used to hear from some of my fellow students in the students' crew room. I used to hear others talking about how brilliant they had been on sorties and I used to think to myself that they were obviously doing better than I was; how wrong I was and it just goes to show that one shouldn't necessarily believe everything that one hears. I learnt from that experience. We were also given our postings and I was absolutely delighted to be told that I was posted to the Lightning, the first RAF supersonic fighter. Of the 26 students on my course, 27 Gnat Course, I think there were six of us who were posted to the Lightning, one was posted to the Hunter, seven or eight to the Canberra and the remaining nine or ten were all posted to become co-pilots on the Vulcan or Victor.

Other things that I remember about my time at Valley were Rhodesia declaring UDI which resulted in one or two Rhodesian students disappearing off the scene at short notice when they had to leave the RAF. I also remember playing lots of sport and having a county hockey trial for the Anglesey team. I even captained one of the teams in the trial. And, finally, I remember one day when the tannoy had announced an aircraft emergency and we had, as usual, gone outside to watch the aircraft in trouble approach and land. On this occasion the aircraft in trouble, a Canberra, had had a bird strike and shut down one engine. We watched the aircraft on its final approach when all of a sudden it appeared a little low. The pilot obviously then tried to increase power on the good engine when, suddenly, the aircraft began to roll, presumably because of the asymmetric effect from the one good engine. We all thought that the aircraft was going to crash and we turned and started to run because the aircraft looked like it was heading straight for us. The pilot must have then reduced power because the wings levelled, he retracted the undercarriage to reduce drag and belly landed, just on the airfield. It could have been much worse.

I was to return to Valley as an instructor some years later but I now left for the next phase of my training, on the Hunter at RAF Chivenor in Devon, with nothing but happy memories of my time on the lovely island of Anglesey during this phase of my training.

CHAPTER 4
INTO FIGHTER COMMAND

Pre-Lightning Training on the Hunter

After finishing my advanced flying training, in February 1967, I then held for a few months before starting my pre-Lightning training on the Hunter at RAF Chivenor on the coast of north Devon. The months of holding were not wasted. I first went to the Lightning base at RAF Wattisham in Suffolk where Nos. 29 and 111 Fighter Squadrons were based. I was now in the new world of Fighter Command, exactly where I wanted to be and I had a great time. I saw just how lively life was going to be on a front-line fighter squadron and I got to know the pilots, all great chaps. Although I was only at Wattisham for three months I worked alongside the officer commanding Operations Wing, then Wing Commander John Tritton, himself a well-known Lightning pilot. I had so much fun and I was made very welcome on the squadrons and in the bar of the officers' mess. The social life was very active and enjoyable and I remember becoming very friendly with the daughter of one of the officers at the base. There were so many there with whom I was to get to know much better in the years that followed and who I still know to this day. Lightning pilots are a unique group of pilots and there is a very strong bond between all those lucky enough to fly this iconic aircraft.

In April 1967 I had to move on and I was desperate to get back in the air as soon as possible. I managed to arrange a short refresher course for myself at RAF Manby in Lincolnshire, flying the Jet Provost again for just a few weeks before reporting to my Hunter course at Chivenor. I completed a short 20-hour refresher flying course which I greatly enjoyed and, after flying the Gnat, I really found it easy returning to the Jet Provost. Even though I was technically still going through my training eventually to become a fighter pilot I was delighted when the squadron commander wrote in my logbook in the end of course summary 'a very competent pilot with exceptional potential'.

I really felt that I was on my way.

I loaded my little white Mini with my worldly belongings and drove to RAF Chivenor. I was at Chivenor from the end of May until early September 1967 during what was a lovely British summer. I was certainly in the right place to be, and at the right time. There were some great sandy beaches in the local area, beaches such as those at Woolacombe and Saunton Sands. The sporting facilities were excellent, life on the base was good, the social life as well, and the flying was just brilliant.

There were about ten students on my course including two officers from the Chilean air force and a couple of qualified flying instructors who were returning to the front line after an instructional tour. Most of us had completed our advanced flying training on the Gnat but there were two who had completed a course on the Vampire. The majority on the course were completing a pre-Lightning course but a few were destined to remain on the Hunter. Although we were, effectively, all on the same course, there were some phases of it which were specific for those going on to the Lightning whilst we did not complete certain phases which were specific to those remaining on the Hunter. The course was conducted on No. 63 Squadron which itself was one of two squadrons that made up No. 229 Operational Conversion Unit. The aircraft we flew were the two-seat Hunter T7s for dual sorties but mainly the single-seat Hunter F6. Compared with the Gnat the Hunter seemed a big aircraft but its performance was not dissimilar to that of the Gnat. However, the major difference was in the capability. I was now going to not just learn how to fly the Hunter but I was going to learn how to operate the aircraft as a fighter, and how to use the weapon capability. I had to understand that the art of learning pure flying had been completed when I left the training world and from now on I had to grasp that flying the aircraft had to become second nature because the really important job of being an operational pilot is learning how to use it as a weapon of war.

The ground school phase was short by previous standards and there was also a simulator to assist with training. It was not long before we were in the flying phase of the course and there was plenty of flying to be done. The flying conversion to the aircraft was also short, a few dual sorties to reach solo flying standard, a few sorties to prepare us for an instrument rating test, a quick formation and night-flying check and then we were well and truly in to the tactical flying phases. We learnt all about battle formation and how to look after all other members of the formation, i.e. how to protect their six o'clock, both in two, and four, aircraft formations. Battle formation became the bread and butter of our day-to-day operations. We learnt how to use the gunsight to track other aircraft and, in these exercises, we would take cine film which could then be assessed and debriefed back on the squadron. We learnt how to use the gun for air-to-air gunnery and we would fire the guns at a moving banner target which was towed by a Chivenor-based Meteor. We were taught all about basic combat manoeuvres, basically how to use the aircraft in a dynamic air-to-air combat environment. We flew one versus one air-to-air combat sorties, progressing to two v one, one v two and two v two combat scenarios. Although the Hunter did not have a fighter radar, we learnt intercept tactics through the use of plotting charts in place of the radar and speaking with ground-controlled intercept controllers based at a nearby radar station. We found out how to be economical with our radio transmissions and how to communicate using minimal use of the radio but in a way that would quickly and clearly convey important operational messages, and information. I absolutely loved all of the flying and I knew that I was in my element, that I was going to become a fighter pilot, of that I was becoming increasingly confident. Becoming an operational pilot is a way of life and it suited me well, I felt like a round peg in a round hole.

I remember so well the students and instructors at Chivenor. On my course there were those who were coming on to Coltishall with me to fly the Lightning – Dave Roome, the first chap who I had met on arrival for officer training at South Cerney; Dai James, who had come through training with me at both Acklington and Valley, Merv Fowler, Graham Clark, Derek Nicholls, an Oxford University graduate nicknamed Chrome Dome because of his bald head. I remember, he had a lovely MG C which one weekend he was demonstrating to a fellow student in an acceleration test down the runway. Unfortunately, he misidentified the distance-to-go markers and went off the end of the runway at 120 miles per hour, destroying a few runway approach lights in the process. Oh well, these things happen!

Unfortunately, both of the course members who had come from Vampires failed to meet the standards required and departed training at Chivenor but went on to slower aircraft roles in the RAF. They both had successful careers in the RAF and beyond and one of them, who had a particularly impressive background education, not to mention one of the finest brains, rose to the very highest levels in the RAF and later became a peer in the House of Lords.

Our time at Chivenor, however, was not without incident and accident, and there were two involving members of my course. One involved my good friend, Dave Roome. He ejected from his Hunter when he experienced an engine failure. He landed safely in a tree not too far from Chivenor and I recall that he surprised an amorous couple who were in the woods at that time, lucky people. I was airborne when the accident happened and was diverted to St Mawgan in Cornwall for the night, returning to Chivenor the next day. When we arrived at St Mawgan, I remember being told that we were in luck because a bus load of Swedish nymphomaniacs was visiting the officers' mess that evening; if only! The next day I led a pair of Hunters on the return trip to Chivenor, both of us students, myself and Derek Nicholls, who were trusted people, a fact that we appreciated. We were increasingly being treated as grown-up people and embryo fighter pilots.

The other accident was less pleasant and involved a very good personal friend, Trevor Sharp, a university graduate who had done well in his flying training. He was a highly intelligent man and an absolute gentleman, one of the nicest people that I had met. Unfortunately, he died in an accident during an air-to-ground weapons training sortie, a tragedy which affected us all. I will never forget the thoughts that went through our heads in the crew room when, first, we wondered why he had not returned from a mission and, then, the realisation that there had been an accident, followed by the sad news that he had died in the crash. It was horrible, there are no other words to summarise our feelings. It was the first but by no means the last time that I was close to such tragedy and it is never pleasant. In that hot 1967 summer, there had also been one other Hunter accident on one of the other courses. In that accident there had been one ejection and one fatality. For those of us in the flying world, particularly in those days, accidents happened and it was an accepted part of the risk. It was also nothing compared to the losses experienced by our heroes, my own father included, in World War II and, in the background, we never forgot their sacrifices.

I mentioned earlier that the social life was good, it was, and there was no shortage of lovely girls to get to know. In particular, I met a very nice girl, Sue Goodwin was her name, her father ran the Barnstaple Club as I recall. We had fun and I kept in touch with her for many years but I was in no way ready to settle down and was continuing to enjoy my bachelor life to the full in every way. That time in north Devon was just wonderful and full of those 'lazy, hazy, days of summer'.

But there was so much more that was fun at Chivenor. On Saturdays we used to always meet at The Three Tuns Pub in Barnstaple, the meeting point for the fighter pilots from Chivenor and the social elite from the town. From those lunchtime drinks the rest of the weekend was normally shaped, usually involving a fair amount of debauchery.

I remember the old man on my course, Derek Bridge, driving his falling apart car into Barnstaple. Whilst stopped at a railway crossing a herd of cows passed by, one of them leant on his car and the whole front wing fell off – the joys of being a fighter pilot! And then there was my, still to this day, good friend, David Matthewson. He had an MG B and I will always remember him saying to me one Saturday afternoon, "Come on Rick let's go to Ilfracombe I want to find a millionairess for a wife". He is still a bachelor and so I assume that he is still looking but, ladies, I assure you that he has always been, and still is, very eligible. Cheques to me please!

The course came to an end at the beginning of September 1967, I obviously passed and was once again delighted to come first in the overall order of merit. At last I was now going to fly the Lightning.

At Last, to the Lightning

"I was always keen to be a fighter pilot and kept saying so."

Above, the words of Al Deere, an outstanding Spitfire pilot in the Battle of Britain, reflect my sentiments exactly.

It was always my ambition to fly the Lightning. It was the final piece of the jigsaw before I was posted to my first front-line squadron. On completion of my Hunter training at Chivenor I moved on to No. 226 Lightning Operational Conversion Unit (OCU) at RAF Coltishall in Norfolk, another well-known wartime fighter airfield. However, before going there we first had to attend a one-week aviation medicine course at RAF North Luffenham, in Rutland, where we were kitted out with the special flying kit that we needed to fly the Lightning – such as a pressure jerkin and g suit – and received intensive training on how to pressure breathe. All of this was necessary because we were going to fly an aircraft that could not only fly very fast, up to Mach 2 or close to 1,500 miles per hour, but also had the ability to fly to a very high altitude. We needed to be trained and prepared for the possibility of experiencing a cockpit depressurisation at very high altitude where, if you were not properly equipped or trained, you could die very quickly. As well as the high-pressure breathing, we also experienced hypoxia and decompression training in special aviation medicine training facilities. It had been a good week and excellent preparation for the flying that was to come, and we were now keen to start our course at Coltishall.

RAF Coltishall was a great place. Situated about eight miles from Norwich, close to the Norfolk Broads, I was just so pleased to have arrived at the home of the Lightning, my dream aircraft for so many years. It really was like fulfilling an aspiration and, over the coming years, little did I know at that stage just how much time I was to spend at the base or how well I would get to know Norfolk, not to mention the lovely ladies from that part of the country.

There were three training squadrons at Coltishall, in those days called Nos. 1, 2 and 3 Squadrons. Nos. 1 and 2 Squadrons flew the Lightning F1A and T4 and No. 3 Squadron the Lightning F3 and T5. Conversion to the Lightning was carried out on No. 1 Squadron and this was followed by basic weapon training on No. 2 Squadron. At the end of that training decisions were made as to where you were to be posted, to one of the Germany squadrons, equipped with the Lightning F2 and T4, or to be earmarked for a UK squadron or squadrons based in Singapore and Cyprus, all equipped with either the Lightning F3 or F6.

My course was small by comparison to my earlier courses, there were 12 of us but only seven or eight were there to fly the aircraft, others were to train as simulator instructors. Course members included seasoned fighter pilots posted to the Lightning from other operational aircraft, or from staff jobs. One was a South African called Ty Retief, I remember him well. He had even flown in the Korean war. We learnt a lot from pilots like Ty, both in the squadron crew room and the officers' mess bar. Most on my course had either been at Chivenor on my pre-Lightning course on the Hunter or on another course at Chivenor at the same time, Dave Roome, Dai James, Graham Clark, Merv 'Masher' Fowler, Derek 'Chrome Dome' Nicholls and Dave Hemmings. We bonded together like a band of brothers. The course started in September 1967 and finished in February 1968, lasting for five months. There was a lot to learn in a short time.

On the first day of the course, we went through the arrival procedure and were immediately made very welcome, and I recall that there was a most enjoyable welcome beer call at the end of the day. However, I also remember that we were all given a familiarisation flight on that day and this certainly 'whet the appetite'. I can honestly think of no better way to start a course. This was the life! That first flight was with my allocated instructor for the conversion phase of the course, Gerry Crumbie. We clicked as an instructor/ student team from that first flight and we were to become good friends. Gerry, as well as being a qualified flying instructor, had just completed an operational Lightning tour at RAF Leuchars on the famous No. 74 Squadron, the squadron that had so much inspired my original desire to fly the Lightning. Gerry was a kind man and also a good squash player. I too had become an accomplished squash player and the daytime flying was often followed by a game with Gerry. Also, since my family were in South Africa, it was too far to go home for Christmas. Gerry invited me to join his family at their lovely house in Surrey and I was made exceedingly welcome. Gerry did not stay in the RAF for a full career and left to become a commercial pilot. He sadly died of cancer in his 50s, far too young, a very good man.

What do I remember of that first flight? Well, my recollection is of the sheer size of the aircraft. It weighed 20 tons and, standing next to it, you realised just what a large aircraft it was, two mighty engines, swept wings and a small cockpit at the front of the aircraft. Gerry did much, but not all, of the flying on that first familiarisation sortie. The sortie comprised start-up, taxi, a reheat take-off and, as I recall, it was what is called a rotation take-off – sheer power, a powerful acceleration, lift off, undercarriage up, 240 knots in no time at all, stick back in the stomach and the aircraft rotates into a vertical climb. Wow! We then reverted to a more normal climb – 450 knots converting to Mach 0.9, level at 36,000 feet after only a few minutes, accelerate to 1.6 and zoom climb, then back to subsonic speed and a recovery back to base through the dive arc. Once back at the lower levels a few aerobatics and then a run-in and break followed by a couple of circuits and then the final landing, chute out, clear the runway, taxi back to dispersal and shut down, a sortie of little more than 30 minutes duration. I was hooked and could not stop smiling.

After that first memorable day there followed weeks of intensive study interspersed with time in the simulator before we started, in earnest, the flying phase of the course. Progress was fast and my first solo on the Lightning followed after just four conversion sorties, and that was yet another memorable day – to be flying solo this magnificent, high performance, very large, fighter, aged 22. I took to the aircraft like a duck to water and I felt very much at home from the start. The Lightning had delightful flying characteristics and to me the biggest challenge was keeping up with the speed of the aircraft and the pace at which you completed tasks. During the conversion phase of the course we explored the complete subsonic and supersonic flying envelope of the aircraft. It was during this phase that we all became members of the 1,000 mph club, at the time a very select club which entitled you to wear a prestigious 1,000 mph tie, and we also received a special certificate to celebrate the date of joining the club, in my case it being 24th September 1967.

The two Avon engines were very powerful and performed well at all altitudes. At low level the speed was restricted to around 650 knots, this was because of the design of the engine air intake and the possibility of engine surge. At high level, where the air is much thinner the Lightning could perform at speeds up to Mach 2.0, twice the speed of sound, and this could equate to speeds well above 1,000 mph. We flew the aircraft up to its height ceiling which was 56,000 feet. However, this height restriction was there to reflect the performance envelope that had been officially cleared during flight testing. Everyone knew that the Lightning was capable of reaching far greater heights and I doubt that there are any Lightning pilots who have not flown the aircraft much higher than this during their time on the aircraft. In my case, the maximum height that I went to was 64,000 feet but I know of others who have been to 70,000 feet and higher. The Lightning has even been known to surprise one or two U-2 pilots at over 70,000 feet. It is a different world at those heights, you see the curvature of the earth and the higher you go the darker it becomes. The indicated air speed can be very low even though you are still going very fast, you sometimes felt as if you were flying on a knife edge and the aircraft, and in particular the engines, needed to be treated with great respect. Although you were capable of climbing to 50,000 feet and above at subsonic speeds the way we would mainly reach the highest levels was through a boom and zoom technique. At the tropopause, usually about 36,000 feet, we would move the two engines into full reheat and accelerate the aircraft from Mach 0.9 to up to Mach 1.6, or even more, and then convert the speed into height. This was the quickest and, operationally, most efficient way of reaching the required altitudes.

The conversion phase also included formation flying, both close and battle, low- and high-level navigation, and instrument flying leading to an instrument rating test. Night-flying took place during the basic radar phase of the weapons conversion. Our aircraft conversion to the Lightning was quickly over and in no time at all we moved on to the weapons phase of the conversion.

In the basic weapons phase the learning was mainly focused on exploring how to execute fighter intercepts at subsonic speeds, flying at 36,000 feet and at Mach 0.9. The airborne intercept radar was known as AI 23 and was a pulse radar. The target pick-up ranges varied at different heights and at 36,000 feet you were lucky to see a target beyond 25 nautical miles. Flying at Mach 0.9 with the target flying towards you at a speed of Mach 0.8 the closing speed was rapid and you had only a short period of time to execute your intercept satisfactorily. During the intercept process, you first had to see the target on the radar and then watch the movement of the 'blip' over a few miles. You were not only flying the aircraft but you had to operate the radar. You had to use mental arithmetic to confirm or calculate target heading, and more, and you had to know what you had to do successfully to prosecute the intercept, aiming to roll out behind the target, in his six o'clock, at an ideal range of one mile. To do this you had to fly the aircraft accurately. Remember also, the Lightning was a day/night and all-weather fighter and you were training to intercept an aircraft that you supposedly could not see other than on radar. As I have said, you had to think fast and you had to have the mental capacity to carry out all of the above in a very short space of time. In the basic phase of the weapons training we learnt all about intercept geometry, learning in a progressive way, from the intercept of targets on known headings and gradually increasing the speed and complexity of the intercept environment. We also completed the night-flying part of our Lightning conversion during the basic radar phase when you could make good use of the darkness both to fly the aircraft and continue to operate the weapons system. The more demanding and advanced intercept training was still to come, where we would also start to operate in a more tactical environment and working more as a formation. I continued greatly to enjoy my Lightning conversion and, as I now entered the final phase of training my desire to reach an operational fighter squadron was rapidly becoming a reality. With regard to my progress, previous tests had always shown my mathematical aptitude to be by far my best academic skill and so I was not exactly surprised that I found myself able to cope with the basic radar phase without too much difficulty.

Before commencing the third and final phase of the Lightning conversion, the advanced weapons/radar phase, we were given our future postings, obviously subject to completing the course. I was delighted to be earmarked for one of the Lightning squadrons in RAF Germany, the famous No. 92 Squadron. This also meant that I remained with No. 2 Squadron and continued to fly the Lightning T4 and F1A. The training was now much more orientated towards preparation for the German theatre of operations. This phase, as you would expect, took the operational training to the next level with more advanced intercept work including subsonic against targets with unknown headings and heights, an introduction to those against targets employing electronic countermeasures, supersonic and high-level intercepts training and the execution of the visual identification of targets.

The visual identification of targets might sound easy to you, the reader, but remember that we had to carry out this work in all weathers, at varying speeds and by day and night. To do this we used our radar to carry out the intercept and then, with the radar still locked on to the target, convert our attention to a head-up pilot attack sight to complete the identification with a controlled approach to the target, closing progressively from one mile to a position 300 yards behind the target before then finding a way to complete the visual sighting. The sun, moon, cloud, to name some of the environmental considerations, all played their part depending on whether it was day or night or in all weathers.

The final phase of the course was demanding and exercised one's mental capacity. I continued to thrive in the environment. My final sortie on the course, known as a tactical evaluation (Taceval) was conducted in an operational scenario where I was on the ground and 'on state', ready to scramble to intercept whatever was directed my way. I was scrambled initially to intercept a supersonic target, the intercept that not only happens the quickest but which also uses the most fuel and requires good sortie management. For example, the fuel gauge on the Lightning, as all those who have flown this magnificent aircraft know, would not infrequently become the most looked at instrument in the cockpit towards the end of a sortie! The Lightning drank fuel! Anyway, my final sortie was successful and it included more than just a supersonic intercept against an unknown target, but against other targets and included the need for visual identification of targets, all conducted in a hostile tactical scenario.

Although we had all worked hard on the course to reach graduation standard – and my own hard work was once again rewarded by coming first in the overall order of merit – there had also been time for play at the weekends. I also played a lot of squash and represented the station team. There was so much to do in the local area, on the Norfolk Broads or in places such as Norwich, and there was no shortage of female company for those of us who were bachelors, and that was most. I do remember one particular party in the lovely village of Horning. At a point during the evening a game of 'Blast Off' was played. This is basically a drinking competition where we all had a pint of beer and a liqueur glass filled with a clear coloured liqueur. The game began with a countdown followed by someone shouting "Blast Off", then you drop the liqueur into the pint of beer and drink as quickly as possible, the first to finish being declared the winner. Well, on this occasion, all was fine for most of us apart from my good friend, Dai James. Somehow, his liqueur glass was not full of liqueur but fairy liquid. He realised that something was wrong when he started to foam at the mouth. He was rushed to hospital and, fortunately, made a full recovery but not before his stomach had been pumped.

The student/staff relationship at Coltishall was outstanding and it was so good to be on a fighter base amongst, and alongside, highly experienced fighter pilots, many of them household names within the RAF from their various achievements. The chief instructor was a great fighter pilot and leader, George Black, and he led the flying side of the station in exactly the way in which I expected to be led. He was, and still is, a very impressive leader, a man to whom I and many others have looked up to throughout our own fighter pilot careers.

The end of my Lightning conversion course marked the completion of training in preparation for joining my first operational squadron. It had taken three years to the day and had been a truly memorable experience. I felt privileged and honoured to have come so far in what was really a very short time for what we had achieved. In the process, I had got to know some of the most beautiful counties in the UK – Gloucestershire, Northumberland, Anglesey, Devon and Norfolk – and also met many new friends. However, it most certainly was not the end of my training. I was now about to embark on the next exciting phase of my RAF and flying career and this involved yet more learning. In fact, as all those who have served as aircrew in the RAF know only too well, you never stop training or learning.

CHAPTER 5
MY FIRST OPERATIONAL SQUADRON

In February 1968, fresh out of the training machine, I was thrilled to be joining my first operational squadron, No. 92, which was very famous for a number of reasons. The squadron had a very distinguished history and was a top-scoring squadron in the Battle of Britain and World War II. Those who served on 92 included household names such as Bob Stanford Tuck, Roger Bushell, Brian Kingcome and Geoffrey Wellum, all famous World War II pilots, all of whom served on the squadron during the Battle of Britain. In the 1960s the squadron also provided the famous Blue Diamonds formation aerobatic team, flying the Hunter and led by Squadron Leader Brian Mercer, later to become a good friend. I knew that I was joining a squadron with an illustrious history. I was also in awe of those pilots already there. Most of whom had been operational Lightning pilots for a number of years, I very much looked up to them as pilots of great experience and from whom I could learn the real art of being a fighter pilot. I joined the squadron the week after it had re-located from RAF Geilenkirchen, also in Germany, to its new base, RAF Gütersloh.

RAF Gütersloh, located in North Rhine-Westphalia, was a German-built airfield, opened in 1935 during the pre-war period. The Americans captured the base from the Germans in 1945 and in the same year it was handed over to the RAF. During the Cold War Gütersloh was the closest Royal Air Force base to the East-West German border, and you knew it. No. 92 Squadron was one of two Lightning squadrons at Gütersloh, the other was No. 19 Squadron. These two all-weather air defence squadrons were a part of the 2nd Allied Tactical Air Force in Western Europe and were responsible for the policing of the British Sector in the northern half of Germany in what was known as Sector 2. Sector 1 was the southern part of Germany and was policed mainly by the US. Also based at RAF Gütersloh were two Hunter fighter reconnaissance squadrons (Nos. 2 and 4 Squadron), a helicopter support squadron (No.

18 Squadron) equipped with the Wessex, an RAF Regiment squadron, a Bloodhound missile battery and a number of other co-located units. Being on the closest RAF operational station to the East-West German border, and one of four fighter squadrons on the base, you needed no reminding of the importance of the base in the Cold War environment. It also provided for an amazingly active social life when off duty. My work-play ethic was about to be very well satisfied over the next three years.

No. 92 Squadron was equipped with the Lightning F Mk 2 which was armed with Firestreak heat-seeking missiles and two (with a capability to carry four) 30-mm Aden guns. In support, there was also one two-seat Lightning T4 aircraft, used for pilot check sorties and instrument rating tests which was also a fully operational aircraft. Average sortie lengths were short due to fuel usage. Subsonic sorties rarely lasted longer than 50 to 55 minutes and supersonic lasted for as little as 20 to 25 minutes. This was a limitation. However, during my tour on 92 the squadron re-equipped with the Lightning F2A which was basically a Mk 2 Lightning which had been significantly upgraded to carry a large fuel tank, known as the ventral tank, improved engines and other aerodynamic improvements. The main and substantial effect was an increase in the average length of sorties to one hour 15 minutes subsonic and 40 to 50 minutes for supersonic sorties. Using fuel conservation measures, sorties could be extended to in excess of two hours. The squadron had an establishment of 12 aircraft plus one T4 although we often had a few spare aircraft in addition which we found invaluable. The Lightning, at times, was not the most serviceable aircraft and, to fix a problem, an engine would often have to be removed to allow access to parts of the aircraft. When I used to walk through the squadron servicing hangar, I marvelled at how the engineers used to, literally, take the aircraft apart and then put everything back together again for us pilots to fly. The engineers worked very hard, day and night, and I greatly respected their efforts. They were very much unsung heroes. We would fly day and night, often until three or four in the morning to complete the flying programme and the engineers would then work until the very early hours to fix snags and ensure that there were sufficient aircraft for the day flying programme the next morning. Weekend working was also not uncommon for the engineers, as the squadron always had to be able to provide sufficient aircraft to meet NATO and operational requirements, 365 days per year and 24 hours per day. The ability to meet these strictures was frequently tested, usually at two or three in the morning. Also, there were always two aircraft on five minutes readiness on 'Battle Flight' but more about that operational task later.

The pilots on the squadron were a truly great bunch and many if not most have remained personal friends throughout my life, and it is now over 50 years since I joined No. 92 Squadron. I remember clearly to this day the names of the pilots on the squadron when I arrived: 'Robby' Robinson, the boss, was a test pilot who had also flown the U-2. The flight commanders were Chris Bruce who later commanded No. 92 Squadron and retired as an air commodore, and Ian Thomson, a great character and a proud Scot who retired as a group captain. Other names that I remember so well were Doug Aylward, who was one of the first three first tourist pilots to be posted to the Lightning. Doug was also my mentor during my initial months on the squadron, an excellent man; Jerry Bowler who was later killed flying as a Red Arrows pilot; Colin Armstrong, who was also killed a few years later when flying as a Red Arrows pilot; Dave Cousins who it was obvious was an officer destined for high rank – rose to become Air Chief Marshal Sir David; John Rooum who went on to become one of the first RAF pilots to fly the Phantom and eventually retired as an air commodore; Hoppy Richardson who went on to become a test pilot; Ed Stein, the squadron qualified flying instructor; John Woolf, another interesting character who, the year before I joined the squadron, had accidentally shot down a Jindivik unmanned aircraft instead of the flare being towed behind it during a missile-firing exercise over the sea, in a designated range for such firings in Cardigan Bay. Years later, and after he had left the RAF, he died in tragic circumstances; Sandy Davis, another proud Scot and a good linguist who went on to fly both the Phantom and the Tornado F3 and who also completed a tour as aide-de-camp to the Air Officer Commanding No. 11 Fighter Group, headquartered at the home of the old Fighter Command, Bentley Priory; Paddy Roberts, an experienced ex-Hunter pilot who was later to become a Red Arrows pilot; Geoff Denny who was the squadron qualified weapons instructor; Jack Glass and David Matthewson who, like me, were the most recent additions to the squadron and who were both first-tour pilots.

However, most of the above pilots had been serving on the squadron since it first arrived in Germany in 1965 and over the next year there was a big changeover of pilots as they moved on to other flying and staff appointments. Therefore, I probably remember, even better, the new pilots who arrived on the squadron and with whom I flew and socialised for most of my tour on 92. These included my second boss, Ron Stuart-Paul who rose to high rank and retired as Air Marshal Sir Ron. He was very loyal to his pilots. The new flight commanders who arrived during my time on 92 were Roger Palin, a Cambridge graduate and Cambridge Blue, a talented all-round sportsman, and who it was also obvious was destined for the top. He had a brilliant career and retired as Air Chief Marshal Sir Roger; Jerry Brown and then Kit Thorman were both very experienced fighter pilots.

Other pilots were Roger Chick, an experienced Lightning pilot and a qualified flying instructor and John Spencer, another very experienced fighter pilot who filled one of two qualified weapons instructor positions and who later commanded the Lightning base at RAF Binbrook and retired as an air commodore. In my early days he took me under his wing as his 'number two', and taught me a lot about being a fighter pilot. The other qualified weapons instructor was Rich Rhodes, a fellow South African and an old boy of Bishops in Cape Town, a rival school of mine. He went on to become a test pilot and then, after retiring early from the RAF, had a very successful career in the aerospace industry. Other names include Pete Chapman, a qualified flying instructor but on his first tour on Lightnings. He had been a 'creamed off' instructor at RAF Valley when I went through there as a student. He was a super chap, a very good pilot, great fun and good company. After a second tour on Lightnings he then flew the Jaguar and, after leaving the RAF, he became a Boeing 747 captain with Cathay Pacific; Graham 'Pritch' Pritchard, an experienced Lightning pilot and a most likeable character who went on to fly in commercial aviation; and Jonathan 'Paddy' Pyper, known as 'Cyclops' because of the 'focused' look from his eyes. He spent many years flying the Lightning. However, probably his greatest claim to fame is that he is married, and consort, to the Lord Lieutenant of West Sussex, his wife, Sue.

Pete Hitchcock was a tall man, who flew the Lightning, Phantom and Tornado and took over from me some years later as the Officer Commanding No. 65 Squadron which was also the Tornado (Fighter) Operational Conversion Unit. Peter also ejected from a No. 92 Squadron Lightning but that happened after I had left the squadron; Norman Barker, a second tour Lightning pilot who ended up a golf club secretary after retirement from the RAF; Vic Lockwood, another great character who went on to become a test pilot before continuing to fly within the aerospace industry; Euan Black, a very talented and natural sportsman, who is godfather to my son and our paths were to cross throughout our careers in the RAF. We served together on other squadrons and he followed me into a number of appointments. He retired as an air commodore; John 'JB' Bryant was the smallest pilot on the squadron but packed a mighty punch for a little man, a great character, they all were, without exception. After two tours on the Lightning he became a Jaguar pilot and commanded a Jaguar squadron, He retired early from the RAF to pursue other interests and was also an airline captain with KLM; 'Furry' Lloyd, a talented guitar player who flew the Lightning for many years and also completed an exchange tour in America flying the F-15. He died of natural causes far too early and while still serving in the RAF; Mike Johnson, a great chap who flew both the Lightning and Tornado F3 and who, for many years, has owned and run a very successful computer business. Over the years he has also run his own wine business and a restaurant; Pete New, who went on to become a Boeing 747 captain with British Airways; Dave Moss, known as 'Moses' and who sported a typical RAF moustache for which the RAF is famous. He retired as a group captain and then became the chief executive, known as clerk, of a City of London livery company; Jim Watson, who left the RAF early and became a captain in commercial aviation; Graham Ivell, who went on to become a qualified flying instructor on the Gnat but who, very sadly, died in an aircraft accident whilst on a sortie over Wales; Tex Jones, another character with an RAF moustache who had previously ejected from a Gnat; and finally, Nigel Adams, who, as I recall, was the last pilot to arrive on the squadron before I left for pastures new.

As can be gleaned from the above information, not all of those mentioned are still living but those that are remain very much a 'band of brothers'. Those that had the ability to fly the Lightning invariably had the ability to succeed in almost any walk of life. At the time of serving on No. 92 Squadron a large proportion of those mentioned above were bachelors, at least two-thirds of the squadron were first-tour pilots. It was therefore a young squadron and we had a lot of fun. The married members of the squadron, and their lovely wives, all seemed to really enjoy the presence of so many bachelors and the squadron social life was very active, to put it mildly.

I mentioned above that we were a 'band of brothers' because that is exactly what we were on the squadron. There were only 15 pilots, we flew together as formations – two aircraft, four aircraft or more – all the time and we learned to place great trust in each other. We not only worked closely together but we socialised together and all this led to a great squadron spirit, an essential ingredient for a successful squadron. Based in Germany, our homes were mainly back in the UK, mine was in South Africa, and so it was only natural that we forged such a special social environment when (far) away from the home environment. The other Gütersloh squadrons and units were the same and, as well as socialising within our own squadrons, we also all met together in places such as the officers' mess. Memorable days indeed!

For my initial months on the squadron I was a non-operational pilot and my first task was to work up to limited combat ready and then combat ready status. This usually took four to six months. Once limited combat ready I was then able to sit alert on Battle Flight and once fully combat ready I was a fully operational pilot and was then able to take part in all operational flying commitments. I was ready to go to war. Consequently, I had to hone my skills in all forms of intercept training, high and low level, supersonic and very high fliers, and against electronic countermeasures (ECM). Very importantly, I had to be able to carry out the visual identification of other aircraft by day and at night, lights out. We learnt how to deal with evasion and air-to-air combat became increasingly important, whether one versus one, two versus two or many versus many. There were many operational procedures to learn, for example how to deal with intruders, survival scramble procedures and much, much more. We would fly mainly within our allocated flights on the squadron, one week on days and the next on nights. The squadron task required that at least one-third of our flying had to be at night.

Gütersloh was required to keep two Lightnings at five minutes readiness to scramble, 24 hours per day and 365 days per year. The aircraft were housed in a purpose-built hangar and was known as Battle Flight. Scrambles were very frequent and we were certainly kept on our toes. We never failed to meet the requirement to be airborne within five minutes, day and night. We were, in fact, often airborne in under four minutes or, if we were already in the cockpit, in under two minutes. No notice operational scrambles, at any time of the day or night, were common. The East-West border was very close and so was the opposition, as their air bases were located close to the border in East Germany. The two sides were effectively little more than 50 miles apart and there was a fair amount of testing reaction that took place. We would be scrambled towards the border because aircraft had been detected heading in that direction. We might reach the border and, indeed, a kink in the border might have been breached by the aircraft from the other side, but only for a few seconds. We would usually end up with opposing aircraft each patrolling our respective sides. However, probably the majority of scrambles were the result of light aircraft either being lost or entering the buffer zone, an intentionally sanitised area created to protect aircraft from straying over to the other side. The intercepts that followed were invariably interesting because the light aircraft would be flying at around 100 knots and our minimum speed was closer to 180 knots. However, when a light aircraft sees a large fully armed fighter pass close by, they get the message and we used to get their tail number which was then reported to the authorities. The pilot of the offending light aircraft knew he was in trouble. Talking about these scrambles, I must make mention of the 'brass monkey' call. All pilots flying in 'western' airspace in Germany were required to listen out on an emergency frequency.

If an aircraft was detected to be in the buffer zone or heading towards the border then an immediate brass-monkey call was put out on the emergency frequency. On hearing this call it was an immediate instruction for all pilots to turn on to a westerly heading and establish their position.

We normally spent twenty-four hours on Battle Flight. This was also a good time to catch up on other things. We could go to bed, and most of us would remain in full flying clothing, but we had to be ready to react immediately because scrambles could and did come at all hours of the day and night. You never knew what was going to happen or when which made it all rather exciting and real. Scrambles were most often towards the border but could be for other tasks, maybe to intercept a friendly aircraft for a number of possible reasons, or perhaps even on a mission to fire a missile in the designated range over the sea. Practice scrambles also took place, usually to facilitate a change of aircraft on Battle Flight or just to keep us sharp.

Exercises were very regular, NATO exercises, 2nd Allied Tactical Air Force exercises, UK national exercises and station exercises. Two o'clock in the morning always seemed to be the favoured time. Some exercises were simply aircraft generation type exercises to test our ability to meet NATO or other requirements. Others were integrated war training exercises moving through the various phases associated with the preparation for war to actual war, from a period of tension phase through to conventional war and ultimately into the nuclear war environment. All front-line bases also had to be prepared for no notice tactical evaluations, known as Tacevals. These examined all aspects of war preparedness and were a major test of a station's capabilities. Taceval was therefore a very important exercise which was fully assessed. Any deficiencies were highlighted and a full report produced. No-one liked to be exposed as deficient but this did happen, but not at Gütersloh which was always well prepared and achieved high marks. We were always at a high state of alert.

There was also one special exercise for which we trained and that was the policing of the Berlin Corridors. If the corridors were closed then the plan was to send a transport probe down one of the corridors accompanied by fighter escort. These corridors were the only way to connect with West Berlin and it was very important that the means to reach Berlin were protected. This was a commitment shared between the United Kingdom, United States and France. Each year, the three nations held an exercise, usually at an air base at Fassberg near the border, to practise the tri-partite contingency plans, and also to better prepare pilots for an actual event. A UK squadron would normally join us for this exercise, No. 5 Squadron as I recall, and it was yet another fine opportunity for international bonding. The Germans were not allowed to police the border. The reality of these contingency plans was brought home in 1968 when the Russians invaded Czechoslovakia and closed the Berlin Corridors. I was on Battle Flight at the time and we were quickly brought to cockpit readiness but not scrambled. The two aircraft on Battle Flight rapidly became ten as the station reacted to what was developing into a very serious situation. We were ready to escort 'transport' probes down the corridors to Berlin, exciting stuff for a young 23-year-old fighter pilot. Fortunately, however, with hindsight, the politicians won the day and the corridors were reopened. Who knows what might have happened had that not been the case.

Turning to day-to-day training, as I have already said, we flew day and night and, certainly during my time at Gütersloh we often didn't finish flying until three or four in the morning. Compare that to these days! In my early days in Germany, as stated most of our training was intercept training carried out mainly in the middle or higher airspace, subsonic and supersonic intercepts, high fliers, and against targets employing electronic countermeasures. However, as the F2A started to be delivered at the end of 1968, with a greater capability than the F2, and as the threat evolved more and more training was carried out at the lower levels. Low-level search patterns were introduced which were manned by a number of Lightnings and the training became much more exciting. The aim was to counter, visually or on radar, aircraft at the lowest levels and to prosecute intercepts and attacks using both our missiles and guns. Some targets were at heights which made it difficult to complete a missile strike and so, for a successful mission we carried out bunted guns attacks from above the target. The low-level search patterns proved to be very effective. All of the previous training remained a part of the syllabus. Of special note, a 'Dial a Lightning' system was introduced whereby other aircraft operating at low level in our area could notify their availability for intercept. This was a very popular and useful training medium.

Supersonic training used to take place over land and above 36,000 feet and the sound of supersonic bangs was commonplace at Gütersloh. Another useful training vehicle was known as Exercise Freelance. If on a training sortie you were left as the only aircraft you could declare yourself to the ground-controlled intercept (GCI) station as available for Exercise Freelance. Intercepts were various but airliners were often on the receiving end, with their permission granted. Also, air-to-air combat training (ACT) and air-to-air refuelling (AAR) were introduced, another important increase in the overall capability of the Germany Lightning squadrons. Finally, training with other NATO nations was a very important part of our preparedness for operations, at all heights and including dissimilar air combat. Training with other NATO nations from all sectors was very relevant. Recovery to Gütersloh at the end of a sortie was always a rapid event with the fuel gauge becoming a major part of any instrument scan. If recovering from height this was done through the traditional Lightning dive arc where we would often find others in wait for us. The area around the dive arc became known as MiG Alley. With regard to weapon training, missiles were fired at missile practice camp detachments to RAF Valley or direct from a Battle Flight scramble. We used to fire the guns once every so often, into the sea off the Dutch coast. The aircraft would shake and you sometimes found yourself with a radio or instrument failure, the result of vibration.

My shortest Lightning sortie took place whilst at Gütersloh, lasting just 12 minutes, and that was in the bigger Mk 2A aircraft. The sortie was a one versus one air combat engagement with my good friend, John Bryant. It was a good fight! When we returned to the squadron operations room the squadron commander, Ron Stuart-Paul, came in and said to us, "Haven't you two walked for your sortie yet?' To which we replied, "Sir, we have just returned from the sortie". I recall that he was somewhat surprised and even suggested that we might have exceeded the time allowed for the use of reheat; we hadn't!

I had a few emergencies whilst on No. 92 Squadron. I only had one fire warning and then the warning light was only on for a second; there was no fire. I did, however, have a fire about which I wasn't aware until after I had landed when the ground crew informed me of the damage to the spine of the aircraft. It had happened after I had fired a missile in the designated range and was in an area of the aircraft where there was no fire detection. Fortunately, the fire had not spread. I also had at least one engine failure and a few other system failures but I had no major emergencies.

I have so many very happy memories of my first tour on 92. They say that your first squadron is always your favourite squadron and that has certainly been so in my case. There are so many stories to remember from these happy three years of my life but perhaps I could summarise some of my feelings.

Girlfriends

I was a bachelor throughout my time in Germany, it was certainly a life that suited me and I was having a great time. I did not feel ready to settle down and at that stage I was intent on staying a bachelor until I was at least 30. That was my aim, time would tell.

I went out with a lot of girls during my tour on 92, there was a lot of opportunity to socialise with the opposite sex. I did in fact go out with one girl for longer than most, let me call her 'H' to protect her identity. She was a lovely young lady who I grew to like a lot and, who knows, it might have lasted for longer but for one situation that arose. That happened whilst the squadron was detached to RAF Brüggen for three to four months. Whilst there, we used to fly for seven days per week and individually we would work for eight days and then have four days off. This was to give those who were married a decent amount of time at home during their days off. I stayed at Brüggen a lot but, on this occasion, I returned to Gütersloh, partly to attend a dinner at the home of H's parents. Another female RAF officer who was based at Brüggen asked me if I could give her a lift to Gütersloh and I obliged. When we arrived at Gütersloh in the early afternoon neither of us had any commitments until early evening and so I invited her into my dwellings to have a cup of tea or a drink. We were sitting there innocently chatting away when there was a knock on the door, I said, "Come in" and H's father opened the door and said something about the dinner that I was going to the following evening. At that dinner he did not say one word to me, not even welcome, and I thought that was strange. On the Monday I was returning to Brüggen after breakfast and whilst at breakfast I was summoned to take a call from H. She said that she wanted to see me immediately and before I departed. I agreed to see her and a little while later met her on the steps of the officers' mess. She simply walked up to me and slapped my face. I was more than a little surprised and asked why she had done that. She responded with, "You know jolly well" and stormed off. Basically, it was because her father thought that my intentions with the other girl were different than was reality. Well, that single event did not end the relationship but it very much influenced any thoughts I might have had about any longer-term involvement.

Camaraderie

This, quite frankly, was probably the most important of my memories. The bonds that were built at Gütersloh were very special and those of us still living remain in good contact. The wives and girlfriends were also an important part of the environment and fully contributed to the life of the squadron.

Whilst we worked hard during the weekdays there was invariably time for play at weekends. There were many squadron parties, in addition to the more official squadron dinners. The married quarters at Gütersloh all seemed to have basements with several rooms. These were often turned into individual cellar bars or party rooms and were the scene of some particularly memorable parties. I was well known for falling asleep and I can remember waking up from one such sleep in a cellar bar after a party. I woke up in this particular cellar bar at about noon only to find that I was locked in the basement. It was at the home of Sandy Wilson, a great friend who became Air Chief Marshal Sir Andrew. Sandy was then a flight commander on one of the Hunter squadrons, No. 2 Squadron. He used to host some great parties in his cellar bar. On this occasion, he got a tremendous surprise to hear a knocking coming from the basement and to then find me on the other side of the door. We have laughed together about that incident and for that matter about other events and antics in which we found ourselves involved whilst at Gütersloh. Parties were always full of fun and invariably went on until the very early hours.

On occasions, groups from No. 92 Squadron would spend weekends in other parts of Germany or visit the surrounding countries such as Belgium, Holland and Denmark. A weekend back in the UK was also an option. The weekend itself would usually start at around five p.m. with the customary Friday happy hour in the 'Kellar Bar' in the officers' mess. This was a downstairs bar with German character drawings on the walls. There was also a special 'Honkatorium' in the associated toilet area. This, like the drawings on the walls, was a relic of the days when Gütersloh was a Luftwaffe base. There was always plenty of inter-squadron rivalry evident at these happy hours, a fair amount of beer used to be consumed and silly games played. I think I will leave it there!

The officers' mess at Gütersloh was also famous for Göring's Room, a room housed within the tower of the building. In this room there was an oak beam which could be collapsed. The story goes that when Hermann Göring would be briefing his men in the room he was reputed to say, "If I am not telling the truth then let the roof fall in". One weekend, a junior officer took it on himself to modify one of the oak beams in the room so that it would partially collapse when a switch was operated. That is the story, the truth is sometimes questioned.

Living in the officers' mess was fun in itself and we were very well looked after in all respects. The accommodation was pretty good, individual rooms were in a series of buildings which stood apart from the main area of the officers' mess. We called them blocks. I had a very spacious room and opposite my room lived another Hunter pilot who became a good friend, John Thompson. John was a super chap, also a pretty good prankster, I recall, and it was obvious that he was an officer destined for the very top and he would have achieved the top position if he had not suddenly died at the early age of 54 whilst commander-in-chief of RAF Strike Command. By then he was Air Chief Marshal Sir John. We were good friends from our days at Gütersloh right up to the time of his death, he was a great man and a true gentleman. John Thompson is an excellent example of the quality of the people at Gütersloh whilst I was there, many went on to reach high rank or to achieve success in the outside world. It was the people who made the place tick. Whilst at Gütersloh, I was also delighted that there were no fewer than 13 officers, including myself, who I classed as South Africans. It felt very much like home from home. During my three years there I was also delighted to see a number of people from my South African days visit the base; my brother, John, together with Wilf Mole, two of my past girlfriends, Liz Swan and Prue Morris, Penny Harrison and Ron Samuel to name some of them. I know the visits were memorable to them for the spirit that they saw and enjoyed.

There are so many more great people that I would like to mention, I remember them all, and I am sorry if any of them read my story and wonder why they are not mentioned.

Squadron Exchanges

Squadron exchanges were a very important part of squadron life. A number of squadron aircraft and pilots supported by ground crew and other personnel would be detached on exchange with another squadron within the NATO environment. At the same time, aircraft and pilots plus support personnel from the exchange squadron would be detached to Gütersloh and hosted by No. 92 Squadron. These exchanges were incredibly useful for a number of reasons. As a part of NATO, it was very important that we were able to familiarise ourselves with aircraft and personnel, and the modus operandi for the day-to-day operations of other nations. This helped us to understand the capabilities of those with whom we would be jointly involved in NATO operations and to get to know the other nations within NATO. We would fly joint missions together during these exchanges, maybe even fly sorties in each other's aircraft and this too built up an understanding between us. The exchanges were also great fun from the social perspective and invariably it resulted in not only a better understanding but new and long-lasting friendships. Most of the other NATO squadrons seemed to be flying the F-104 Starfighter during my time on 92.

As well as squadron exchanges, we regularly used to carry out joint training sorties with other air forces and land away at other bases within our theatre of operations, the northern part of Germany, Sector 2. We also operated with the United States Air Force squadrons based in southern Germany who were responsible for the southern sector in Germany, Sector 1. All of these initiatives contributed to a better understanding within the NATO environment and also enhanced our operational readiness and mutual understanding.

Bolthole to the 'Clutch'

In 1970, RAF Gütersloh's runway was resurfaced and the two Lightning squadrons deployed to RAF Brüggen and RAF Wildenrath for four months; in the case of No. 92 Squadron we went to RAF Brüggen. Nothing changed from the operational perspective whilst we were on deployment. The squadron continued to operate Battle Flight but from Brüggen instead of Gütersloh and our day-to-day operations remained the same. One big difference was that we carried out training at weekends as well as during the week. The squadron operated for seven days a week. One big advantage of the deployment was that all pilots were living in the officers' mess and this was a major opportunity to enhance squadron spirit, and this is exactly what happened. After what had been a very pleasant four-month deployment, we finally returned to Gütersloh, or so we thought. We departed Brüggen in style, the major element as a nine-aircraft formation, and we made ourselves known both on departure from Brüggen and on arrival at Gütersloh. I recall that I was number eight in the formation and I burst a tyre on landing. The aircraft behind me were immediately diverted to our crash diversion, the German air force base at Hopsten. Well, the boss was just in the process of giving me a king-size bollocking for my burst tyre when the senior engineering officer (SENGO) came up and said that every tyre in the formation was shredded. In short, the landing had felt like a landing on sandpaper and it transpired that the co-efficient of friction for the runway was all wrong. We then spent a week at Gütersloh, mainly in the bar, whilst the engineering contractors worked on the runway. We then flew another nine-aircraft formation to test the runway, which resulted in more burst tyres. That same afternoon the squadron re-deployed all aircraft to RAF Wildenrath from where we continued to operate for another month whilst the runway was finally sorted. This was all very exciting to me as young bachelor, fairly wild colonial boy, with no family commitments. I am not so sure that was the case for those who were married. Also, whilst at Wildenrath I was involved in another memorable experience.

My Royal Experience

In 1970, Princess Anne was planned to visit RAF Germany to present a new standard on behalf of Her Majesty the Queen. Some weeks before the big event I was on a social weekend down at the RAF Germany Headquarters at Rheindahlen, in Mönchengladbach. As I and a good friend, Tim Thorn (known as Tiger Tim), a fellow bachelor, Hunter pilot, and also, like me, from the African continent, were leaving the discotheque in the social club we bumped into another friend, Steve Gruner, who was the aide-de-camp to the commander-in-chief of RAF Germany, Air Marshal (later Air Chief Marshal) Sir Christopher Foxley-Norris, another well-known Battle of Britain pilot. Steve said to us, "Ah, Rick and Tim, how would you like to escort Princess Anne to the Royal Ball that is to follow the standard presentation?" We both had a few beers in our bellies by this time and both of us replied, "No problem, Steve". I thought no more of it until, on the following Monday, I was summoned by my squadron commander, Ron Stuart-Paul, to his office. In his broad accent he said: "I don't know what this is all about Rick but I have had a call from headquarters, something about they want you to escort Princess Anne to the Royal Ball. I told them that they had got the wrong man but they were insistent!" Before the evening, Tim and I were summoned for a briefing by the commander-in-chief. He said to us, "Well, you know why you are here, you have been chosen to escort Princess Anne at the Royal Ball. She will have been with a bunch of old fogeys all day, you will be the VIPs for the evening, make sure that she has a good time. She doesn't drink. I am not saying don't drink just don't get drunk, and don't get amorous." As it turned out, Princess Anne was an absolute delight and good company and we all had a lovely evening. She didn't leave the ball until five thirty in the morning. Since no-one else was allowed to leave before Her Royal Highness it was not surprising to see a lot of the older generation asleep. Tim and I then turned into pumpkins, ceased to be VIPs and ended up walking most of the way back to our base at RAF Wildenrath before a lorry driver came to our rescue. The occasion had been an unforgettable experience. When I returned to the squadron, the next time I went flying I discovered that the ground crew had hijacked my helmet and at the back of it was a badge that said 'By Royal Appointment', a fitting sequel.

RAF Germany Winter Survival Course

In the winter months each year, RAF Germany ran a winter survival school at a lovely German hamlet called Bad Kohlgrub in Bavaria. It was a two-week course for aircrew to gain experience in winter survival and escape and evasion, to prepare us for the real thing should that day ever arise. We stayed in a lovely guest house in the village where the food, beer and company were all excellent. The first week of the course was spent being given lectures on survival and being taught how to ski as a means of making sure that we were at peak fitness ready for the four-day survival exercise that was to follow in the second week. All RAF Germany aircrew were expected to attend this course once during their tour of duty in Germany. In my case I had a double dose because, at the end of the first week, I tore the ligaments in my right knee on the ski slopes and was therefore unable to take part in week two. This meant that I was able to attend again the following year which also meant a second week of free skiing. The survival part of the training was very good indeed and from the start we were put into a real-life operational scenario, what we might expect to find if we had to eject from our aircraft over hostile territory. We were equipped with only what we were wearing and what was available to us from the ejection. This meant that we had to improvise a lot, using our dinghy as a bed, our parachutes as a tent and fending off the land as best we could together with the food and other aids contained in our dinghy packs. We had to move across snow-covered countryside and in a hostile environment. Our training included a proper escape and evasion exercise as a part of the survival training. If you were caught, and most were, we then had the luxury of experiencing interrogation procedures. For safety purposes we operated in pairs and if one person was caught then the other had also to surrender. The interrogation seemed very real and taught me a lot. I won't go through the full details but suffice to say that it included a lot of physical exercise with a sack over one's head plus exposure to a variety of different interrogation techniques. I will never forget the experience and it not only taught me a lot about my own survival capability and resistance to interrogation but it also educated me, once again, just as it had done during my officer training, about the strengths and weaknesses amongst others undergoing the same experience. Most importantly, it taught me that I had a very strong constitution when it comes to staying alive. At the conclusion of this four-day exercise the bath that I had back at the guest house, the first beer and the meal that followed were all wonderful.

My Flame Throwing Experience

This was yet another experience in my life that I will not forget. At the end of a very good evening in the bar in the Gütersloh officers' mess, as used to happen in those days, we started to play silly games. I had already eaten a raw egg and part of a wine glass and now it was my turn to try a bit of 'flame throwing'. Well, the rest is history, I forgot to stop the air coming out of my mouth and experienced burns to my throat caused by what is known as 'blow back'. Three days in sick quarters was the result, no flying and the only relief was provided by my fellow squadron pilots who discreetly were able to supply me with beer for lubrication purposes. Back on the squadron I was summoned by the squadron commander, who expressed his disapproval by telling me in his strongest Scottish accent, "Everyone does something bloody stupid on their first tour, Rick, and you have just done yours… take three extra Battle Flights". I wasn't complaining.

At the end of my three years in Germany (now a 26-year-old bachelor), I was posted back to the Lightning Operational Conversion Unit at RAF Coltishall as a tactical weapons instructor giving airborne instruction to those undergoing training on the Lightning and, in particular, to those destined for the Germany squadrons, just as I had done only three years earlier. I really did not want to leave Germany, it had all been such a fantastic experience but all good things, I guess, had to come to an end. At least I was able to drive back to the UK in my new tax-free BMW 1600 which I had collected from the BMW factory in Munich and which had cost me the princely sum of £740. I was dined out by the squadron before I departed, one final long and very fine evening, during which one of my fellow pilots read out the following words which he had composed:

'We say farewell to Edwards
Old R S P-E
Our colonial wild boy
A splendid jarpie!

A great Amstel drinker
A boozer of style
He'll drink any liquid
Watch out River Nile!

The Ladies all love you
But why we can't say
It must be your shyness
That makes them that way!

You're bound now for Coltishall
To show them we wish
How to fly like a fighter
And drink like a fish!

We'll miss your happy presence
And so will the bar
No more will your laughter
Be heard from afar!

Rick, we shall miss you
We wish you the best
You've been good for the squadron
But we all need a rest!'

CHAPTER 6
A SECOND LIGHTNING TOUR

Full of great memories from my first Lightning tour in Germany I was delighted to be posted for a second tour flying the aircraft at RAF Coltishall, returning to the station on which I had originally completed my Lightning operational conversion course. I already had many friends in the local area.

I joined No. 65 Squadron, one of two Lightning squadrons at the operational conversion unit, as an instructor. The squadron was an operational squadron declared to NATO as a reserve squadron but our main task was to train new pilots on the Lightning and, in particular, all those destined for Germany. I was 26 when I joined and five years, or more, younger than most other pilots on the squadron at that time. This fact itself was something of a new experience coming from a squadron where two-thirds of the unit were young first-tour pilots. The instructors on No. 65 Squadron had a wealth of operational experience, many of them on aircraft such as the Hunter or Javelin before flying the Lightning.

After arrival on the squadron, I initially went through a short instructor work-up before I starting instructing students. The course was very similar to that which I had completed just three years earlier, any changes relating to updates in the ways in which squadrons operated. For example, in the Germany phase of the course there was an increase in low-level intercept training and the use of evasion, and the introduction of more air-combat training. I did a lot of flying during this tour, on many occasions flying four sorties per day. One of my squadron commanders on No. 65 Squadron, Al Blackley, wrote an appropriate comment in my logbook, where he recorded, with my annual assessment of ability: 'This pilot has an insatiable desire to fly!' He was correct. I always felt happiest in the air, and there is nothing to beat the airborne environment, especially flying an aircraft like the Lightning. By the end of this tour I had amassed nearly 1,500 flying hours on the Lightning and in the process flown many more sorties. I have always said that my Lightning instructional tour at Coltishall taught me more about flying than any other flying tour.

The staff/student relationship at Coltishall, as it had been when I was a student, was excellent and we all worked and played hard, very much in line with my personal ethos. During my time on No. 65 Squadron the cadre of instructors changed a lot during the two-and-a-half years that I was there. I was delighted that a number of these were my old colleagues from No. 92 Squadron – old friends such as John Spencer, Pete Chapman and John Bryant were all posted to No. 65 Squadron as was Bob Turbin who had also been with me in Germany but flying with the other Lightning squadron, No. 19 Squadron. He had been promoted to squadron leader and became my flight commander. I was pleased because my character was much more in harmony with Bob's than with his predecessor, and we were very much on the same wavelength. There were many characters among the instructors on 65, names like John Kendrick, a very fine Lightning pilot, and Dickie Duckett, who went on to lead the Red Arrows and then commanded a Harrier squadron. He retired as an air commodore. Peter Bedwin was, like me, far younger than most of the other instructors and we were both very happy that the large majority of those posted on to the squadron were our age. Peter went on to fly Phantoms before leaving the RAF and later becoming managing director of a major aerospace company. Taff Butcher was another great character. He and I enjoyed a healthy competitiveness in the air combat arena and I liked his humour and style. He went on to become an airline captain. Sandy Davis, also of my vintage and who had been with me on 92, has always been a good friend, was another character on the squadron before he went off to become aide-de-camp to the Air Officer Commanding No. 11 Fighter Group. Actually, I too had been shortlisted for the job but, at the time, I knew that I did not want it because it would have taken me away from the flying environment that I loved. Sandy and I had initially been on a shortlist of four before being further down-selected to the last two. I remember that we went down to London the night before the final interview and enjoyed a very late night out on the town. My eyes must have looked like poached eggs at the interview the next morning and when asked whether or not I wanted the job my answer was an unequivocal "No thank you, Sir". I was not selected and Sandy got the job but, now with hindsight, I think that I might have found the job an interesting challenge. Dick Bealer joined No. 65 Squadron towards the end of my tour after a Lightning tour in Cyprus. He had a fairly wild reputation and was a delightful man to know, a fine pilot and a loveable rogue. Brian Carroll had great experience and was like a father figure and was a very friendly, kind man. There were other instructors who I have not mentioned, all of whom were great colleagues. The squadron commander was Wing

Commander Murdo Macdermid, another man of character and who had a rich sense of humour. He liked a good cigar and a glass of whisky and told many a good story.

My students were all good pilots, some better than others. That is what I expected because anyone who arrived to fly the Lightning had, if they were straight out of flying training already come through a rigorous process which progressively eliminated any who were not making the grade. Some of my students going to Germany were already very experienced Lightning pilots posted to take senior jobs – for example, Wing Commander John Mitchell was on his way to take command of No. 92 Squadron and Wing Commander Pete Vangucci to take command of No. 19 Squadron. None of my students who had not previously flown the Lightning failed and a number of them were also posted to Germany: David Cyster, Phil Roser, Rod Sargent, Ray Hodgson, Derek North, Rod Sears and Simon Lloyd-Morrison. I remain in good contact with many of them.

Operationally, we still took part in many NATO and national exercises but there was no Battle Flight/quick reaction alert (QRA) from Coltishall, that task was mainly carried out from other bases. Our role was air defence of the United Kingdom and with other UK squadrons we were responsible for the air defence of the UK Air Defence Region, a very extensive piece of sky around the UK. The operational role was rather different flying in the UK, mainly because we were that much further away from the opposition than we were in Germany and most of our operations were conducted out over the North Sea. We also relied to a much greater extent on what we called 'force multipliers', the use of air-to-air refuelling and early warning aircraft.

There were many notable events in which I participated during this tour, both operationally and socially. From an operational point of view the highlight of my time there has to be when the station was awarded the Stainforth Trophy as the best operational station in Strike Command, a prestigious award and achievement, especially since we also had to deliver on a big student training task.

A highlight for me was taking part in an air-to-air gunnery trial, flying from St Mawgan in Cornwall and making use of the air-to-air gunnery range out over the sea near Lundy Island. It was a memorable week. I flew 20 sorties in just five days, all were gun firing at a banner being towed by a Canberra aircraft. I remember that the week had some interesting moments when the sea fog would start to roll on to the land and St Mawgan was a coastal airfield which could become fogged out very quickly. The timing of our sorties became very critical on occasions. At the end of the week we were able to have a weekend in Devon and Cornwall which was both relaxing and enjoyable.

That was not the only gun firing I was involved in. I also spent a very enjoyable three weeks detached to the other Germany Lightning squadron, No. 19 Squadron, as one of their weapons instructors during their armament practice camp (APC) at Decimomannu in Sardinia. I found this to be a very satisfying task. It was nice to feel that I was back on a Germany squadron even if it was not the one on which I had served. All squadron detachments are enjoyable, particularly if they are overseas, and this was no exception. It was hard work and a great challenge but there was also plenty of opportunity to enjoy the social scene.

Whilst on No. 92 Squadron I had completed an instrument rating examiner course which qualified me to carry out annual instrument rating tests on pilots as an examiner. Whilst at Coltishall, as well as continuing to conduct these tests on No. 65 Squadron pilots, I found myself in demand to also conduct tests in Germany. This meant that I continued to visit Gütersloh on a regular basis. I also used to instruct new instrument rating examiners on their courses.

Lightning emergencies were a common event on the aircraft, for a number of different reasons, and I had my fair share whilst at Coltishall, However, and fortunately, I did not have any major emergencies. Every day there seemed to be two, three or more emergencies declared and announced over the station tannoy. I recall we lost two aircraft on No. 65 Squadron but all pilots successfully ejected. My good friend, John Spencer and his student, Geoff Evans, had to eject after engine surge problems and my old flight commander from No. 92 Squadron, Chris Bruce, also had to eject because of a control problem. They were all successfully rescued from their dinghies in the North Sea. I remember the elation I felt when I heard that John was safe. I had the task of going around to his married quarter to break the news to his wife, Pat, about what had happened but, most importantly, I was able to tell her that he was safe. There was the occasional undercarriage collapse, fire problems, tail chute failures on landing, burst tyres, electrical and hydraulic failures, the occasional engine failure and more. Lightning pilots always had to be ready to react fast to any emergency and, to this end, we were always kept up to speed through our regular simulator sorties.

I remember one occasion when a two-seat Lightning was doing a reheat take-off and the instructor was an American exchange officer. One of the reheats did not light – it was the lower engine, and this made it hard to raise the nosewheel at the usual speed. The instructor said s**t, the student thought that he had said chute and pulled the chute handle, which was immediately shredded by the reheat and the take-off had to be aborted at a late stage which meant a high-speed barrier engagement. The aircraft ripped the barrier out of the ground and would have easily won the Norfolk ploughing championships. It took more than a day to recover the Lightning from the muddy ground. Both pilots were fine but this all happened because of a language misunderstanding.

It was while I was at Coltishall, as I recall, that bachelors were no longer obliged to live in the officers' mess. A fellow Lightning pilot, Trevor Macdonald-Bennett, and I took advantage of the new rule and rented a bungalow in the nearby village of Tunstead. We lived out, as it was called, for much of 1971 and 1972. To us, this felt like real freedom and we made the best of the opportunity. We had a lot of fun although both of us would freely admit that we weren't over-domesticated. We had a lady who came in to clean the house once a week and that normally involved washing up a week of dirty dishes. Trev made it quite plain from the start that he wasn't interested in gardening. I was but, when I saw that this would have involved creating a garden at what was a newly built bungalow, I quickly changed my mind. We entertained a lot and I well remember the first time that it was my turn to do the cooking. I obviously thought that I knew more than I did because I had been given a 'cooking for beginners' book in which there were photographs of all types of food discussed, e.g. if it was an egg then there was a photograph of an egg. Very helpful, too! On this first occasion I failed with my baked potatoes because I had assumed that when the potato was hot then it was ready to eat! Wrong, as we discovered at the dinner table with rock hard baked potatoes. Oh well, one lives and learns.

Whilst 'living out' we also had a very lively holiday in the South of France where we had rented a six-berth caravan in a campsite at a place called Fréjus. We were joined by another RAF Regiment officer, Nick Acons. We drove down to France in Trev's two-seater Triumph sports car and a chance meeting on one of the French toll roads was to make our holiday even more lively. We bumped into Sandy and Lesley Wilson who had been at Gütersloh with me. Sandy was a Hunter pilot in those days. Anyway, we discovered that they were going to the same area, in fact only a mile or two away from our campsite. To cut a long story short, we saw a lot of each other over the two weeks of the holiday and had an even greater time.

At the end of the holiday, we returned to Coltishall via Gütersloh where we stayed with more good friends, Norman and Janet Barker. Norman was a Lightning pilot on my old squadron, No. 92. Back in the UK, we stopped renting the bungalow when Trev left the RAF and headed off to Saudi Arabia to fly the Lightning in that country. I moved back into the officers' mess with nothing but happy memories of a really good time involving two fairly extrovert young bachelor fighter pilots. Before Trev departed Coltishall he got married for the first time and I was his best man. His old squadron commander on No. 74 Squadron, an infamous fighter pilot, Ken Goodwin, had also been summoned to the occasion to give the bride away. That too was a memorable wedding. Trev and I and our wives are still in good contact.

I have so many happy memories of my second spell at Coltishall, I was still a bachelor throughout this tour. I had told myself that I had no intention of getting married until I was at least 30. I wanted to 'play the field' and this I certainly did for most of my 20s. However, I did not last until I was 30 and married my wife, Tina, when I was nearly 29. Tina was posted to Coltishall straight from her training at RAF Shawbury as an air traffic controller. She was just 19. I met her on her arrival at the Coltishall officers' mess on New Year's Eve 1972. I was at the reception desk speaking on the phone to the girl who I was taking out that evening when she arrived. I was immediately interested in this new WRAF officer and went to the bar, to where she had gone to quench her thirst, and introduced myself. For some reason she fascinated me from the start and I was impressed that she was able very much to hold her own in any discussions. I later found out that she had been head girl at school and also won the sash of honour on her officer training course at RAF Henlow and these facts certainly confirmed that she was a strong character. Anyway, it took me the next six weeks to persuade Tina to come out with me on Valentine's Day 1973. She thought that I was too old and resisted my initial advances. However, following our first date, events moved fast and we became engaged in April at a wedding at RAF Wittering. I remember that Tina was then going away for a couple of days and I picked her up from the station in Norwich on her return. She was quiet and I wondered what she was thinking! I said to her in the car on our way back to Coltishall, "Did I ask you to marry me the other day?" To which Tina answered, "yes". I then asked, "And what did you say?" To which I was delighted when she replied, "yes". As for the engagement ring, I didn't have one on me when I had asked Tina to marry me, I had asked her on the spur of the moment. We went to a jeweller in Norwich and Tina said, "How much can you afford to spend?" To which I said, "whatever you want". She got the message and we bought one for £34 which was about equal to the total amount that I had in the bank at the time!

Our engagement was announced in *The Daily Telegraph* but for some reason my letter to inform my parents in South Africa never reached them and the next thing was that I received a telegram from them saying, '*Daily*

Telegraph announces your engagement, please report'. My grandmother in Jersey had seen the announcement and asked my mother questions in her weekly letter to her. Telephoning South Africa in those days was not easy and very expensive but to say that I was somewhat embarrassed is an under-statement. However, the situation was quickly resolved.

We were married the following January in the station church at RAF Valley where her father, Rayner Harries, was the chaplain. He had had to obtain a special licence for the wedding. The wedding was a great day, a gloriously sunny 19th January 1974, Tina's father married us and her young brother, Mark, then aged 12, gave her away. I have never forgotten Rayner's advice to us at the altar: "You are both stubborn people, remember that fact, and never go to sleep on a disagreement without saying sorry." My best man, Jim Ross, had been a search and rescue helicopter pilot at Coltishall and he too was now based at Valley as an instructor on the search and rescue training squadron. We had much in common, we both loved our sport and played very competitive squash with each other and we both liked our beer and the social life. I called him 'Baldy' and he called me 'Fatso'. We remained good friends over the years but, unfortunately, Jim died in 2017. His son, Ben, a policeman in the Royal Military Police, had also been tragically killed in Helmand Province during the Afghanistan conflict, yet another victim of an improvised explosive device. Tina and I attended his very moving funeral at his old school, King's Bruton, in Somerset.

I flew Tina in a Lightning before we were married, much to the surprise and hilarity of the safety equipment staff who had the task of kitting her out and preparing her for the flight. They were first interested to hear that she was flying with me and asked if she knew what she was letting herself in for. They then noticed her engagement ring and when they discovered that she was engaged to me, they were filled with hilarity. I must add that Tina herself tells this story better than I.

A few other memories from my wedding day: a very good friend, Dick Doleman, who was the deputy senior air traffic controller at Coltishall had bet Tina £5 that she wouldn't get me down the aisle and so she won the £5 which to this day sits proudly framed at home. Dick was also heard to say in a loud voice at the back of the church as we became husband and wife, "He's gone". As for my bachelor party, all I will say is that I managed to survive the experience. We stayed for our wedding night in the lovely town of Dol-gellau in north Wales. I remember, as we arrived, the manager asking if we were just married to which I gave a negative answer. It was the wrong reply, he would probably have given us a complimentary bottle of champagne if I had given a positive answer and, in any case, I was dripping confetti at the reception desk.

I also remember very well another event that happened whilst on my Coltishall tour. On Saturdays, we bachelors would disappear off to Norwich for a pub lunch and on one particular occasion we continued our celebrations at the Norwich Rugby Club before returning to the officers' mess. Then someone said that there was a party on that evening at RAF Wattisham and why didn't we go down there for the evening/night. Well, we did and we also had a very lively party which led to an exchange of phone calls on the following Monday between the respective presidents of the mess committees, the senior job in the mess. To cut a long story short, some months later, on returning from a night away at Gütersloh, I was met on the aircraft apron after landing and informed that the station commander wanted to see me. I knew why! I entered his hallowed office, saluted and was asked what I was doing that weekend. I said, "Nothing Sir" to which the station commander replied: "Good, because if you were then you're doing something else now. Since it seems like you like parties and since it seems like you like going to other stations, you are now to go to RAF Uxbridge where you will be staying with the Air Officer Commanding of the Military Air Traffic Organisation, a well-known aviator and party lover by the name of Air Commodore Bertie Wootten, and you will be escorting his daughter to the Uxbridge Summer Ball." She was a lovely girl and great company and I had a memorable stay, easily the best punishment that I have ever had!

Coltishall was a very lively place to be based, right next to the Norfolk Broads. I well remember how us bachelors from the officers' mess, staff and students, would go boating on a Sunday afternoon. Two of us would first go to Wroxham to hire a boat while everyone else waited to board down at the Rising Sun pub in Coltishall village. Someone was also usually delegated to pick up a barrel of beer from the mess plus glasses and then a pleasant after-noon was had by all. It was certainly a most pleasant way of socialising and seeing some of the most beautiful parts of Norfolk, and it was a great way of spending a Sunday afternoon.

I left Coltishall and the Lightning in mid-1973 and I can honestly say that I enjoyed every single one of those hours. The Lightning was, and remains, a very special and iconic aircraft to many more than just those who flew the aircraft. I was very privileged to fly it for six years, my dream had come true, and I will always be a very proud WIWOL (stands for 'When I was on Light-nings'). The affectionate term WIWOL came about because people would say that you could never meet a Lightning pilot without being told very shortly thereafter about time spent flying the beast.

CHAPTER 7
AS A QUALIFIED
FLYING INSTRUCTOR

At one stage, at Coltishall, as I waited to hear about my next posting, I was told that I had been shortlisted for the first tranche of pilots chosen to fly the new Jaguar aircraft that was about to enter service but instead I found myself destined for the Central Flying School, at RAF Little Rissington in Gloucestershire, to become a qualified flying instructor on the Gnat. Although most of our ground training at CFS was done at Little Rissington all of my flying was done from Kemble where the Red Arrows were also based. As the end of my second Lightning tour approached, I was constantly reminded because everywhere you went at Coltishall you would see the words 'RPE for CFS'. People knew that I did not want to leave the front line.

Now I will say right up front that, whilst it was true that I went kicking and screaming to become a flying instructor, the experience was 100 per cent positive and it was very rewarding, I loved the flying, and I thoroughly enjoyed my time in the flying training world.

I joined my course at RAF Little Rissington in June 1973 and graduated just before I got married at my new base, RAF Valley, in January 1974. There were about 30 of us on the course, destined for various training aircraft, the majority to instruct on the Jet Provost whilst others were going to the Varsity, Bulldog or, as in my case, to become a qualified flying instructor on the Gnat. The course began with an intensive ground school phase for the first couple of months before we commenced the flying phase. I was one of four pilots earmarked to fly the Gnat, three of us were destined for the Advanced Flying School at RAF Valley and the fourth member, a Saudi Lightning pilot, Ghazi Darwish, to return to instruct in Saudi Arabia. Of the three of us going to Valley I had joined the course from the Lightning, one of the others, Mel Cornwell, came from a Phantom F4 reconnaissance squadron and the other pilot, Dan Walmsley, from the Canberra. We went through our instructor training at the time of the oil crisis in 1973. As a result, flying hours were limited and we therefore did not carry out any preliminary flying at Little

Rissington on the Jet Provost before commencing our time on the Gnat. I therefore found myself with nearly a month free after the ground school phase before commencing the flying phase on No. 4 Squadron at Kemble. Surprise, surprise, I went back to Coltishall to do a little more Lightning flying and of course there was the added attraction of Tina, my fiancée, still being based at the station.

I really enjoyed flying the Gnat again, a real little sports car, and I liked even more flying from RAF Kemble. We used to travel daily between Little Rissington and Kemble in a rickety old bus driven by a legendary driver who was quite a character and had been doing the job for years. We would depart from Little Rissington early in the morning and return usually just in time to shower and change for dinner. The overall atmosphere at Kemble was superb and, in many ways, it felt like a flying club. The boss was Guy Whitley, a great character, and the instructors – all of whom had already completed instructional tours on the Gnat – were all good chaps; Ross Payne, who had been flying Lightnings with me in Germany but on No. 19 Squadron; Ed Jones and Ian Reilly, both ex-Canberra pilots and who went on to fly the Jaguar, and Derek Fitzsimmons who went on to become a member of the Red Arrows team. The Officer Commanding Operations Wing at Kemble was Wing Commander Sid Edwards, a friendly man with a good sense of humour who kept us laughing in the crew room with his wealth of stories. We all worked hard and, at appropriate times, we played hard. The flying was intensive. After re-familiarising with the Gnat, we quickly found ourselves in the instructor training phase. We had to learn every aspect of the sequences to be taught at Valley, from the initial effect of controls through to the more advanced high level, supersonic, low-level navigation and formation phases. Also, everything had to be taught as laid down in the instructor's handbook. The usual routine was that I would fly a sortie with one of the instructors, in my case that was usually with Ian Reilly or Derek Fitzsimmons, and he would 'give' me the instructional sequence with me as the student. I would then fly two mutual sorties with one of my fellow course members. On one of these sorties I would practise giving the instruction to my colleague and on the other sortie we would reverse roles. I would then fly a fourth sortie which was a 'give back' of the instructional sequence to the instructor. Every instructional sequence involved a routine of four sorties. There were a lot of instructional sequences to learn and I got plenty of flying on the course. At the end of the instructor course, just before I was to move on to RAF Valley, I had a big surprise and a difficult decision to make.

One of the Red Arrows pilots had lost his medical category and was therefore temporarily grounded from his flying duties. I was approached, through the squadron boss, by the then leader of the Red Arrows, Ian Dick, and invited to become one of their pilots. The problem that I had was that I was about to get married, Tina and I had just bought our first house on the island of Anglesey and we were booked to go on honeymoon to South Africa for three weeks. All of this would have had to be put on hold. I would have loved to fly as a member of the Red Arrows aerobatic team but, at this time, I did not think that it was an appropriate way to start my married life and I, therefore, very reluctantly declined the offer. About 18 months later I had another, similar, offer to join the team when a different pilot member had also been temporarily grounded for medical reasons. This time the offer came from a different leader of the Red Arrows, Dickie Duckett. He and I had served together on No. 65 Squadron where, as well as his instructional duties, he had been the Lightning aerobatic display pilot. I used to fly his spare Lightning to most of the air displays and we also played a lot of golf together. He was a very fine golfer and was RAF champion on at least one occasion. I was also a useful golfer. However, on that occasion the RAF answered the question on my behalf. The reason why I was unable to accept the offer on this occasion was that I was about to be promoted squadron leader and become the deputy chief instructor at Valley. I always had a desire to be a Red Arrows pilot but I guess that it was not to be, as they say 'so near and yet so far'. Nevertheless, whilst at Valley, I regularly flew with the team, including with the synchro pair, on training sorties and to this day I have always had a close association with them.

On completion of my instructor training at Kemble I graduated as a qualified flying instructor. However, because of the oil crisis we did not have any of the usual end of course gatherings and even the graduation dinner was cancelled. We simply moved on to our respective flying training schools.

I had three years at No. 4 Flying Training School at RAF Valley and I loved every moment. I enjoyed being an instructor on the Gnat, I was in the early years of my marriage and living in our first house, albeit with a 100 per cent mortgage. My fellow instructors were a great bunch of chaps many of whom I already knew from our time flying the Lightning.

My station commander at Coltishall, the then Group Captain (later Air Chief Marshal Sir Joe) Gilbert, a great commander and leader, had helped secure a posting for Tina to become the first female air traffic controller at RAF Valley, and I am not sure that her new boss, at least initially, fully approved of a female on his staff. However, she quickly showed herself to be one of the very best air traffic controllers and she was extremely popular with both the aircrew and her colleagues in air traffic control. She more than proved her value and so much so that when, after about 18 months, she became pregnant and had to leave the WRAF, as they did in those days, she was given a special surprise on her final day at work, with a flypast of five Gnats and four Hunters over the air traffic control tower in a 'T', for Tina, formation. She fully deserved this unique accolade.

I was an instructor on No. 2 Squadron at Valley and progressed rapidly up the chain. I quickly achieved a B1 instructor category and then became an A2, which means above average, instructor at the first attempt. The A2 re-categorisation requires a lot of study because, as well as a challenging flying examination, there was an equally comprehensive ground examination, of both knowledge and instructional technique, to pass. My examiner was actually an old friend, Derek Fitzsimmons, who, of course, had been one of my instructors at Kemble before becoming a Central Flying School examiner, affectionately known as 'Trappers'. The fact that we knew each other well, believe me, did not score me any advance points. The overall examination was a real test of my ability and I felt justifiably elated when I was told that I had passed. The next stop was to the bar! On No. 2 Squadron I became a deputy flight commander not long after joining the squadron and then, just as rapidly, I became a flight commander. I relished the added responsibility.

My fellow instructors on No. 2 Squadron were a really nice group of pilots. The squadron commander was Squadron Leader Jerry Dawes, a real gentleman and a person who I liked a lot. We used to share similar interests and I have always felt a little guilty for one day, after a few beers, showing him a shortcut out of the officers' mess when the back door was closed. Unfortunately, when he jumped down from the relevant window, he broke his foot. There was some explaining to do to his wife not to mention at work. He left the RAF not long after leaving Valley and ended up flying for the Sultan of Brunei. In retirement he settled in Australia but I enjoyed dinners with him and his lovely wife, Ines, during their annual visits to the UK. I succeeded my old friend and fellow Lightning pilot, Dave Roome, as a flight commander when he was posted back to the front line to fly the Phantom. My co-flight commander was initially Roger Taite, a helicopter pilot and a true gentleman and, when he moved on, he was replaced by Graham Mackay, a former Vulcan pilot who went on to become a fighter pilot on the Phantom. They were both really excellent chaps as were all of those who were my fellow instructors on No. 2 Squadron: Gordon Young, Brian Todd, Mike Keane, Stu Price, Paul Barton, John Cheyne, Bob Lindo, Richie Thomas and Frank Foster are names that immediately come to mind.

My time as a flying instructor I found both satisfying and very rewarding. Although I had already had experience of being an instructor on the Lightning, I learned a lot about students in this job. In particular, that you could not, as I said I would do before I started to instruct, turn every student into the 'best on the course'. Each of my students had their own strengths and weaknesses, and individual abilities and capabilities. Any deficiencies would quickly become evident. For example, events happened fast in the Gnat and flying the aircraft would quickly expose any lack of mental capacity or ability to cope under pressure. However, my aim, always, was to work with my students to achieve success and to see them complete the course and progress to the next stage of their training. I believe they all knew that I was very much on their side. I enjoyed getting to know the students and seeing the course spirit develop. There were some tremendous characters and some very talented individuals. Many of them became and remain good friends.

Two years into my tour at Valley I was promoted to squadron leader and became the deputy chief instructor. In that capacity I had much added responsibility and worked closely with the chief instructor, initially Wing Commander John O'Neill and then Wing Commander Boz Robinson, both of whom I got on with very well. In that job I flew both the Gnat and Hunter, and with all three of the training squadrons at No. 4 Flying Training School, two of which flew the Gnat and the other the Hunter. I also spent two months as the caretaker squadron commander of one of the Gnat squadrons, No. 1 Squadron, yet another very satisfying experience.

The flying, as I have already said, was exceptional. It was also plentiful and by the time I next moved on I had very quickly amassed over 1,000 hours on the Gnat. The opportunity for low flying, in particular, was of special note and I flew low-level sorties all over the UK. The low flying in Wales and Scotland was particularly memorable because of the spectacular scenery and the opportunity to fly down deep valleys, over undulating countryside and over beautiful lakes. I used to do rather more low flying than most because I had qualified as a pilot navigator instructor after completing a very enjoyable and testing course.

The social life was equally good and Friday happy hours in the bar in the officers' mess were always lively nights. Living and working so far from the bright lights of London meant that the social life blossomed. In many ways, the liveliness of the station was not dissimilar to my experiences on a fighter base but then that was not altogether surprising because many of the instructors were themselves fighter pilots. There was a lot to do on

Anglesey and in every way, it had been yet another memorable three-year flying tour but not without sadness.

A lot of flying took place from Valley and flying accidents happened. During my time on Anglesey a number of aircraft were lost in that way, two Hunters and three Gnats, as I recall. Eight pilots were killed. A two-seat Hunter hit a hill in Shropshire and the instructor and student were killed. A single-seat Hunter had an engine failure after a display practice, the aircraft was not in a position successfully to complete a forced-landing at Valley, or at any other airfield, and the pilot successfully ejected and was rescued by helicopter. Two Gnats with four instructors on board had a mid-air collision at low level over Wales and all four instructors died in the accident. Finally, another Gnat, with an instructor and student on board, stalled and crashed during a turn on to the final approach at RAF Shawbury and both pilots were killed. Another two-seat Hunter landed fast at Valley after a practice forced-landing and the aircraft got in to what is known as a pilot-induced oscillation (PIO); the aircraft then bounced down the runway like a porpoise and came to a halt at the end of the runway with a collapsed undercarriage. The pilots were unhurt. One never likes any accident happening and fortunately, as the years go by, the number of them has been progressively reduced and are today very rare.

I cannot finish this chapter without making mention of the location of my house, which was situated a quarter of a mile on the approach to the main runway at Valley. In those days, Valley was open twenty-four hours a day as a master emergency diversion airfield. There were aircraft movements day and night and we were often shaken out of bed at three o'clock in the morning by a Vulcan or an American F-111 overshooting the runway in full power. You would think that I should have known better but we did buy the house on a 'quiet' Sunday. Also, if it wasn't aircraft noise waking us up at that time of the morning, then it was one of our cats presenting a live baby rabbit to us in the bedroom. I often ended up having to chase and catch these baby rabbits in the bedroom while Tina would lock the offending cat in the other bedroom. Very romantic!

CHAPTER 8
THE MIGHTY PHANTOM

I was away from the front line for three-and-a-half years before returning, in February 1977, to convert to the Phantom. Now, as a squadron leader for another Cold War fighter tour, this time on No. 111 Squadron based at RAF Leuchars in Scotland. The squadron was equipped, initially, with the Phantom F4M until, during the second half of my tour, the F4Ms were replaced with the Phantom F4K which the squadron inherited from the Royal Navy when HMS *Ark Royal* was decommissioned.

On my Phantom tour the air defence squadrons were not only responsible for the air defence of the UK but also, in the absence of any aircraft carrier capability, for the air defence of the Fleet. Exercises were as regular as they had always been. Treble One Squadron (No. 111 Squadron), affectionately known as the 'Tremblers', was the top-scoring RAF squadron in World War II and had also been the home of another famous Hunter aerobatic team, the 'Black Arrows', who, to this day, still hold the world record for the number of aircraft in a formation loop, 22 in all.

Phantom Operational Conversion at Coningsby

Before joining the squadron, I first did a Phantom conversion course at RAF Coningsby in Lincolnshire. Whilst this course should have been a short one, instead we completed a long course to help the system because there was a need to match up a group of mainly first-tour navigators with a group which comprised only ex-Lightning pilots. This meant that instead of a three-month course we were at Coningsby for six months.

Joining the Phantom world was a new experience. After 12 years in the RAF, flying mainly single-seat aircraft, this was the first time that I had flown with a navigator, better called, in my view, either a 'fightergator' or weapon system operator. The way of operation was also different. There was more preparation on the ground before sorties, in the simulator or on the air-intercept trainer, the sortie briefings and debriefings lasted longer than I had been used to on the Lightning, and instead of flying two or three sorties a day we were flying about three or four per week whilst training at the operational conversion unit. Nevertheless, one thing was for certain, the preparation was thorough and the training productive.

The Phantom was a very capable aircraft and had proven itself in conflict. It was a real war machine and, from an operational perspective, was a lot more capable than the Lightning. Like the Lightning, it could fly at twice the speed of sound and well over 1,000 miles per hour. At low level it was limited to 750 knots. The 'g' limits varied depending on aircraft configuration but 7.5 g was the most 'g' that we were allowed to pull. The aircraft was equipped with two Rolls-Royce Spey engines. The engines were very effective at the lower levels, or when supersonic, but tended to run out of puff at the medium to high levels when subsonic. The weapon system was a quantum leap forward. Armed with eight missiles, four heat-seeking and four semi-active radar-guided, they integrated well with the very capable radar. The radar had a number of modes including separate pulse-doppler and pulse capabilities and a ground-mapping mode. We were able to see targets at great range and the ground-mapping capability gave us the option of not only using the radar for navigation purposes but also to carry out internal aids approaches to runways or, for that matter, targets. A centre-line-mounted Gatling gun could also be carried. The gun was an impressive addition with a firing rate of 6,000 rounds per minute. The Phantom was also equipped with an inertial navigation system which considerably enhanced the situational awareness capability. Pilots had a gunsight and it was also my first experience of using the presence of an angle of attack indicator capability to achieve best performance, and on the final approach to land. This too was a most useful aid. There were many other avionic improvements in the cockpits, from the availability of radios including an HF radio to the presence of a radar homing and warning receiver, and more. There was a command ejection capability associated with the ejection seats which could be selected to allow the occupant of either seat to initiate ejection of both aircrew, or to maintain individual control. There were even night formation lights, and we used to practise night formation. The capability of the Phantom was hugely impressive, as one might expect from an aircraft that had a multi-role capacity. Before switching to the air-defence role with the RAF the Phantom had initially been used very effectively in the air-to-ground and photographic-reconnaissance roles.

The syllabus on the conversion course was broadly similar to what had been taught on the Lightning. At the same time, however, it was very different because it was designed around the overall capability of the aircraft, the use of a two-man crew, and to take advantage of the significantly increased length of sorties. The average duration of subsonic sorties was around one hour and 45 minutes and about one hour for supersonic sorties. With the addition of a third fuel tank underneath the aircraft the sortie length could be further increased to two-and-a-half hours or longer. The air-to-air combat phase was much more comprehensive and the course, additionally, included night formation. My back-seater on the course was a first-tour navigator, Tim Hill. I liked flying with Tim a lot, he was, and still is, a great character, noisy in the bar and very competent in the air. He also had the largest collection of shirts of anyone that I have ever met. Mind you, I didn't appreciate it when, flying in close formation one day and in the middle of some fairly heavy manoeuvring, and almost inverted, a voice from the back seat suddenly said, "Check fuel". An expletive followed.

The Phantom also had some interesting flying characteristics which had to be learnt. On take-off, you initially used the control column in the opposite sense from what one expected. When manoeuvring the aircraft under 'g' you did not use the ailerons to turn the aircraft, you used the rudder. If you attempted to use the ailerons when pulling more than 16 units of angle of attack the aircraft would roll in the opposite direction. This was because of what is known as adverse yaw. On landing you did not use the rudder to straighten the aircraft before touchdown, and you did not 'flare' before touchdown, you simply flew the aircraft into the ground and it would then straighten itself to align with the direction of movement. The Phantom had been designed to land on an aircraft carrier and had a very strong undercarriage.

Whilst at Coningsby, there is one day that will remain chalked in my memory forever, 3rd May 1977. Mid-morning on that day, I had been flying on a two-aircraft intercept sortie out over the North Sea and we were on recovery to base. As we approached the coast, I heard a Mayday call over the radio. It was an American voice speaking from air traffic control at RAF Alconbury, a United States Air Force base in the UK. The controller called, "Mayday, Mayday, Mayday, B-67 aircraft [the American equivalent of an RAF Canberra] suspect crashed near RAF Wyton". Apart from the fact that this was the first Mayday call that I had heard thus far in my flying career, I was aware that my first cousin, John Armitage, the son of my mother's twin brother, was based at Wyton doing a Canberra refresher course at that time. After landing, I learned more about the accident and that it appeared there were no survivors. As the day went on, I reassured myself by thinking that no news was good news. I returned home in time to listen to the six o'clock news on which I knew the accident would be the main story. As I started to watch the television the telephone rang and it was my other cousin in the UK, John's sister, Kay. She simply said, "It was John" to which I responded, "Tina and I are on our way". John was living with his mother in a house near Wyton. His father, Jack, was living in Australia and I was the only male close relative in the UK. Within two hours of Kay's call, Tina and I had arrived at his mother's house where we stayed for the next week to help as best we could. Tina was heavily pregnant at the time with our first daughter, Lisa, who was born at RAF Hospital, Nocton Hall, in Lincolnshire just four weeks later. The period after John's death was obviously not a pleasant time but I know that our presence was very important to his mother and sister, and to the wider family, and it was also where I wanted to be. We returned to Coningsby to resume my Phantom training after my cousin and his navigator had been buried at the church in Houghton Village. It was just four months later that I played a part in a happier family event near Wyton. John's sister, Kay, was married in the same area and I was privileged to give Kay away at her wedding in the absence of her father. That was a joyous occasion but obviously still tinged with sadness. Our eldest daughter, Lisa, not yet four months old, was a great attraction at the wedding reception.

No. 111 Squadron at RAF Leuchars

In August 1977, I finally arrived at Leuchars to join No. 111 Squadron and what proved to be a memorable and eventful tour which was to last until November 1980. I should add, however, that for nine months of this tour, in 1979, the squadron 'boltholed' back to RAF Coningsby whilst the Leuchars runway was re-surfaced. The word 'bolthole' was simply a word used for such deployments. It was during this time that our second daughter, Jenny, was born in October 1979 at RAF Hospital, Nocton Hall. I was about to launch on a night land away sortie when I was given the message to rush to Nocton Hall as quickly as possible because Jenny's birth was imminent. I reached the hospital at about five p.m. expecting Jenny to be born at around six thirty p.m. and imagining that I would be able to celebrate later in the bar. Well, Jenny finally arrived at 11 p.m. and it was too late to go to the bar! I was still very elated.

At the end of my tour I had flown over 1,000 flying hours on the Phantom, the third aircraft on which I had achieved this milestone. The others, of course, were the Lightning and the Gnat. I was one of the squadron executives and I filled the positions of the squadron qualified flying instructor and also the executive officer. It was very different from my previous squadron experiences, mainly because there were roughly 44 aircrew instead of the 15 pilots on a Lightning squadron. There were also more aircraft, 15 or 16. To me, it was a big squadron, one of two RAF Phantom squadrons at RAF Leuchars, the other being No. 43 (Fighting Cocks) Squadron. Leuchars, at the time, was also the home of No. 892 Squadron of the Royal Navy and the aircraft and crews operated from the base when not at sea on board HMS *Ark Royal*. It made for a lively station.

Leuchars was a great place at which to be based. Situated on the east coast in Fife, the university town of St Andrews lies on the other side of the Eden Estuary which separates the two places. There was also the luxury of St Andrews Golf Course for any golfers, of which I was one. I was a member of St Andrews throughout my time in Scotland, I played there a lot, and the annual cost was, shall we say, very accommodating. The town of Dundee was nearby and Edinburgh little more than one hour away. There was also a mainline railway station at Leuchars and the beautiful Scottish hinterland was very accessible. It is not surprising that Leuchars has always been a popular place at which to be based. My long-term paternal ancestry is Scottish and there is still a family firm of solicitors located in Edinburgh. I have always loved a lot of what is Scottish, the beauty of the countryside, the mountainous area on the west coast, golf, bagpipes, whisky, the traditions, even the weather – which can be both very bad and very good. There is a lot about Scotland that is endearing.

Whilst on Tremblers I was crewed with three navigators, all of whom I liked. Dave Read, a very experienced back-seater was my first navigator. He and I won a trophy as a top scoring crew at the conclusion of my first armament practice camp on the Phantom. This was conducted from Leuchars in a range off the coast of Scotland shortly after my arrival on the squadron. It was a good start. My second navigator was Pete Hinton. He and I had gone through our initial training in the RAF at more or less the same time. This was his first tour on the Phantom after completing a couple of Canberra tours. We worked well as a crew both in and out of the cockpit. Mind you, one day I thought that he had died on me; we had just had a tremendous low-level hassle with a large formation of Jaguars and Harriers which involved a lot of turning and pulling of 'g'. After the fight had been terminated, I said to Pete in the back seat, "That was good sport, Pete?" Silence. "Pete, Pete, can you hear me?" Silence. After what seemed like a few minutes a voice emerged from the back and said, "What is going on?" I can't tell you how relieved I was to hear his voice again. By this stage, I had already climbed the aircraft to a higher level, called base and set course for Leuchars. I asked for a medical team to meet the aircraft on landing. Pete was taken off to the station medical centre and I began to fear for his flying future if there was a medical problem. As it happened, Pete was back in the air the next day, the doctors deciding that he had fainted because of a low blood sugar level, probably due to a lack of intake of the appropriate foods and liquids before going flying. Pete never had a problem again but it was a lesson learned and it had certainly given me one hell of a fright. My third navigator was a straight through first tourist, Graham Bond and he was also a very nice chap and a competent 'fightergator'. We too bonded well both in and out of the cockpit. A two-man crew can be very effective when the crew works well together, the opposite can also be the case if they do not function properly as a team. I was always very happy that I and my back-seaters were working as a good team.

There was a tremendous group of flying executives on Tremblers. The boss was Wing Commander Gil McCluney, another well-known Lightning pilot, a character. His successor was a navigator, Wing Commander Don Read, a grand man. The flying squadron leaders during my three plus years, and including myself as a member of that group, were Chris Read, Dick Northcote, Euan Black, Mal Gleave, Roly Taylor and Cliff Spink. Most of these names either already were, or became. household names within the fighter fraternity. It was a top team. There were so many aircrew on the squadron that there is not enough space to name them all but I will mention the fact that one of the squadron pilots was an exchange officer from the US Marine Corps. Two of these exchange pilots played a major role in Tremblers during my time. The first was Dave 'Circus' Stamper – a great air combat pilot and a fine squash and golf player – with whom I have remained in good contact ever since. For some reason he refers to me as the 'Earl of Westfield'. He was eventually succeeded by Bill Hauser. They were both excellent pilots and great characters, team players who brought much to the squadron. There is tremendous value in these exchange postings.

The day-to-day operational flying training was magnificent. We had to satisfy an annual syllabus of training activities covering all aspects of our operational role. This included the usual intercept work, at all heights, and with various levels of evasion tactics, supersonics, high-flying targets, electronic countermeasure training, and much more. We did a lot of air-to-air combat training, both against similar and dissimilar aircraft types, and low-level intercept work against aircraft such as Harriers, Jaguars, Buccaneers and many other aircraft from the UK and other NATO countries. Air-to-air

3

1. Teddy Peacock-Edwards (seated left) in Malta in 1941 with 261 Squadron.

2. Teddy Peacock-Edwards in Ceylon during the 1940s.

3. Rick with his mother.

 R.M.M.V. CAPETOWN CASTLE

4. Rick (right) with his brothers John and Mike.

5. Rick as a new boy of Michaelhouse, January 1962.

6. En route to the UK on the *Capetown Castle* in 1965 with Tony Cook and Grant Whitten.

7. At RAF Acklington as part of No. 179 Course. Rick is sitting first on the left.

8. A RAF recruitment poster from 1969 with Rick standing on the steps of a Lightning.

9

10

9. Rick (on the right) sitting next to Princess Anne at a Royal Ball held during her tour of RAF Germany in 1970. Rick's friend, Tim Thorn, is to the right of the princess.

10. No. 92 Squadron missile practice camp, 1968. Rick is to the far right of the group.

11

12

11. No. 92 Squadron Lightning F2a with No. 2 Squadron Hunter FR10 over the Möhne Dam.

12. Rick and Tina's wedding, 19th January 1974. From left to right: Ruth Hayes, Rick, Tina, Murray Hayes (Rick's godfather) and Rick's mother Jill.

13

13. 'T for Tina' flypast of Hunters and Gnats led by Rick to celebrate Tina's last day as a RAF air traffic controller.

14

10 Bear Club

This is to certify that :~

Squ.Ldr. R.S. Peacock-Edwards
in pursuance of his duty to maintain
the integrity of the U.K. Air Defence
Region has intercepted 10 Bear aircraft and has demonstrated to the
Soviets the resolve and skill of
R.A.F. fighter crews.

Date : 21 Apr.'80.

President :

15

14. Rick's Ten Bear Club certificate demonstrating his interception of ten Russian Bears over UK skies.

15. No. 2 Squadron, No. 4 FTS instructors at RAF Valley in 1976. Back row (from left to right): Stu Price, Dave Major, Al Dorey, Paul Barton, Gordon Young, Frank Foster, Brian Todd and Bob Lindo. Front row (from left to right): Graham Mackay, John Cheyne, Jerry Dawes and Rick.

16. No. 111 Squadron in Malta, 1978.

17. A Phantom F4 with a Russian Bear.

16

17

18. RAF Coningsby 1986. Nos. 64 (Phantom) and 65 (Tornado) Squadron emulating a photograph of the two squadrons taken when they were based at RAF Duxford in the 1960s and equipped with the Javelin and Hunter.

19. A unique flypast at RAF Cottesmore of a Lancaster, Spitfire, Hurricane, and Tornado F2.

20. Cold War RAF Fighters: Tornado F3, Phantom and Lightning.

21. The Peacock-Edwards family in 1983.

22. Rick as Tornado F3 squadron commander.

23. Rick and Nobby Clark – the first RAF Tornado F2 crew.

24

24. A synchronised display of a Spitfire and Tornado F2 in 1985.

25. Arriving in Masirah, Oman prior to taking part in Exercise Saif Sareea in 1986.

26. Leading the Queen's 60th birthday flypast, 1986.

25

27

28

27. View from the cockpit during the Queen's 60th birthday flypast.

28. The unique 11 Group multi-formation flypast at Mildenhall in 1986.

29

29. Rick with his mother and wife at Buckingham Palace after receiving the Air Force Cross.

30. Rick as station commander at RAF Leeming.

31. The Peacock-Edward family at RAF Leeming.

32. Princess Margaret planting a tree outside the officers' mess at RAF Leeming in 1992.

33. Handing over command of RAF Leeming to Group Captain Phil Roser in June 1992.

34. Rick as air attaché in Washington.

35. Rick and Tina in Washington, December 1992.

36

37

36. Rick with his toys, 1994.

37. Rick as Inspector of Flight Safety with Air Marshal Sir Ken Hayr, the first Inspector of Flight Safety at RAF Bentley Priory at the naming of a lecture theatre in AM Sir Hayr's honour.

38

39

38. At the Air Pilots Banquet in Cape Town in 2009. Rick is pictured alongside Andy Green, Richard Noble and Tony Ogilvie.

39. HM the Queen meeting Rick, then vice chairman of the RAF Club, in 2012 when the club's trustees hosted a special lunch for 11 members of the Royal family. The Queen had earlier unveiled the Bomber Command memorial.

40

41

40. Rick with Eric 'Winkle' Brown at a lunch held to celebrate Brown's 95th birthday.

41. The Peacock-Edwards family at the wedding of Rick's daughter Jenny in July 2017.

refuelling was a regular addition to our training activities as were operations with the airborne early warning Sentry aircraft. Whether operating over the sea, low flying throughout Scotland, and other areas, the task was just superb and challenging. Although we mainly operated from Leuchars we also used to go on regular detachments to Europe, Cyprus, Malta, Sardinia, to other NATO countries and also within the UK. The flying was both interesting and varied, by day and night. It was often quite demanding and, in particular, training for such vital tasks as visual identification, both by day and without lights at night. For example, carrying out a 'lights out' visual identification on a dirty, dark night, at a height of 1,000 feet over the sea, certainly concentrated the mind. As I have already said, the Phantom was a hugely capable aircraft and a real war machine, and all of our operational training was obviously geared towards just that possibility. The most important part of our peacetime operations, however, was quick reaction alert, known as QRA.

Quick Reaction Alert

In the UK there are permanently at readiness aircraft on QRA to cover both the northern and southern areas of the UK. Northern QRA was mounted from RAF Leuchars with two Phantoms at ten minutes readiness, 24 hours per day, 365 days per year, and scrambles were regular. However, the QRA sorties were very different from what I had experienced in Germany. Most of the intercepts were mainly of Russian Bear and Badger aircraft and took place in the Iceland/Faeroes Gap way to the north of Scotland. The Russian aircraft used to operate or pass through the UK Air Defence Region for a number of reasons. They could be in transit to Cuba, they might be operating with Russian ships on exercise in the North Atlantic, they could be monitoring our own exercises or working with Russian submarines, or they could be practising their war role against the UK. This would likely involve the launch of stand-off missiles aimed at targets in the UK, and from a considerable range. Finally, they would sometimes be found flying near the oil rigs in the North Sea. Whatever their mission might have been, they were entitled to operate in international airspace but no closer to the UK than 12 miles from land, that is where the international airspace commences. The numbers of Russian aircraft would vary and we would react to deal with the amount that we expected. This would sometimes mean that we had many more than two aircraft on QRA. We would intercept and identify any unknown tracks (usually Russian aircraft), have a close look and then shadow the aircraft, until they headed back north to return to their operating bases which were not far from the Arctic Circle. During these intercepts we would work closely with the Americans operating out of Iceland and the Norwegians flying from bases in Norway. We were always supported by tanker and airborne early warning aircraft. We flew long sorties, usually in excess of five hours. As for diversions when operating so far north, we would plan, if necessary, to use small airfields in the Shetlands where the runways were, in all probability, too short for a Phantom. To overcome this problem, certain airfields were equipped with specialist arrester gear so that we could stop by using our tail hooks to catch a wire on landing, similar to landing on an aircraft carrier. During my time on No. 111 Squadron I intercepted over 30 Russian aircraft at all hours of the day and night, and at all heights. It was a rewarding experience. This also qualified me to be a member of the Ten Bear Club.

Incidents and Accidents

I had a number of incidents during my tour. The following are just some of those that I experienced.

The date was 20th February 1978, I was on a night sortie with another Phantom and we had just completed an air-to-air refuelling exercise with a Victor tanker aircraft when the other Phantom went unserviceable and had to return to Leuchars. It was 11.30 p.m. and, at that time of night, there wasn't any other trade with which to work. My aircraft was full of fuel and too heavy for a landing. I decided to do a practice diversion to Losssiemouth in north Scotland.

I carried out an instrument approach to the runway and commenced an overshoot at about 50 feet. As I opened the throttles there was an almighty bang and the sky lit up. I could see immediately that my right engine had seized because the rpm gauge was at zero. I immediately needed to select full reheat to be able to climb to a safe height. I made a Mayday call while at the same time air traffic control told me that I was on fire. There were hot blades coming out of the back of the aircraft via the jet pipe. Fortunately, the reheat lit, I knew then that the aircraft was flyable and downgraded the Mayday call to a Pan call (meaning that the situation was still serious but I was not in imminent danger).

At that point, a voice from the back seat, Pete Hinton, said, "What the f**k is going on?" We were then able again to take control of the situation as a team. It was a very serious engine failure, we landed and once we had sorted the aircraft, called Leuchars to inform and debrief, and completed the paperwork, we went to the night bar in the officers' mess for a much-needed beer or two. On runway inspection, two bags of engine blades were recovered. This incident was probably the closest that I had ever come to an eject situation which we would have had to do had the reheat not lit on the good engine. It was also fortunate that the engine failure was contained and that the blades did not penetrate a shield around the engine. If it hadn't been contained then it would have taken out the other engine as well, also an eject situation.

I had one other memorable engine failure on the Phantom, on 16th October 1980, at the end of a six-hour flight from Akrotiri in Cyprus to Leuchars with my then navigator, Graham Bond in the back seat. The squadron had been on detachment to the island for about seven weeks. Fortunately, the engine failed towards the end of the sortie during the recovery to Leuchars, otherwise I would have had to divert. This engine failure was also not nearly as dramatic as the earlier one and I landed safely after a Pan call. As you might imagine, I was fairly keen to get home to see my wife and children again after so much time away from home.

One other incident that I remember occurred in my formation but not to me. Together with the US Marine exchange officer, we were transiting from Scotland to Cyprus with two tanker aircraft on a 'trail' proving sortie before RAF fighter squadrons again started to use the island for detachments. The date was 23rd January 1978. I was with one tanker in the lead and my number two was with another tanker in trail. We were refuelling over the Mediterranean when the trail tanker aircraft, with its Phantom 'plugged in', hit the slip stream from the lead formation. The result was not very pleasant and ended up with the probe receiver on the trail Phantom being torn off and thus negating the capability to take on any more fuel. Without going into detail, most of the formation continued to Cyprus, and the second Phantom diverted into Malta and flew on to Cyprus later that day with the probe extended after checks had been carried out in Malta. I tell you this story because it shows just how rapidly situations can change and that decisions have to be made quickly after considering the position and weighing-up the options. You always have to be prepared.

Unfortunately, accidents do happen in the flying world in spite of efforts made to prevent such unpleasant events. Fortunately, over the years the number of accidents has significantly reduced and will continue to do so as new technologies are introduced. My time on No. 111 Squadron was marred by a number of accidents and there is no doubt that morale was affected. During my three years and three months on the squadron, the following occurred.

In August 1978, the squadron lost an aircraft and two crew in an accident over the North Sea in a challenging, but not unusual for an all-weather fighter, weather environment. The pilot was a very experienced US Marine Corps pilot with over 1,400 hours on the Phantom and who had recently joined the squadron. He had achieved fame for landing a Phantom during the Vietnam War with most of a wing shot away, a great achievement. However, on this occasion, during an all-weather and all-heights intercept mission over the North Sea, for whatever reason he, together with his back-seater, Chris Ferris, perished in an accident when they crashed into the North Sea. I was the authorising officer for this sortie and, during the subsequent Board of Inquiry, my role in this capacity came under the microscope, and that is putting it mildly. It wasn't pleasant, I was aware of those in the system who were after my blood but I was grateful to those closer to home who protected my position and, in the end, even though not a victory, had secured a compromise position. I was given a reproof, which is a punishment that does not stay on one's career record. To be given the reproof, I was summoned to Headquarters No. 11 Group, at Bentley Priory, where I was given a 'hats on' interview by the then Air Officer Commanding No. 11 Group, Air Vice-Marshal Peter Latham. At the end of the interview I could not wait to get out of the building and back to Coningsby. I rushed down the main corridor only to be caught at the front door by the aide-de-camp to the AOC who said to me, "We thought that you might want to see some of your friends before departing". I replied, "Do I f**k, I just want to get back to my squadron, I just want to get away from here". I was then invited back into the AOC's office for what turned out to be a very friendly fireside chat. My faith was restored because I always felt blameless and that I was a victim of circumstance. However, in the whole process, I, and my family, had experienced 18 months of great anxiety. I am a tough man but there are others, as I had discovered back in my training days, who are not quite as resilient. This raised flight safety questions in my mind which were to return later in my career when I became the RAF's Inspector of Flight Safety (see Chapter 13). Once again, the fabric of my make-up had been severely tested. I must have lost a few stone in weight in the process but I am *not* a quitter.

In November 1978, the squadron lost another aircraft and two crew on a night sortie when the aircraft crashed into the North Sea. This felt like a double blow to the morale of the squadron. The aircraft was a Mk 1 ex-Royal Navy Phantom. The pilot was a very good friend of mine, Chris Jones, an ex-Lightning pilot who had just returned from a course at Coningsby where he passed as a qualified weapons instructor. He was one of the best, as was his back-seater, Mike Stephenson. I am not sure that the cause of the accident has ever been fully explained or confirmed but there was a view at the time that the aircraft might have experienced a double generator failure which, in the absence of an appropriate back-up system, would have meant the loss of all lighting in the cockpit, with disastrous consequences. Chris's wife Dorothy (Dot) is godmother to our second daughter, Jenny.

Later in November 1978 the squadron lost another Phantom although this time the crew, thankfully, survived. In the space of three months we had lost three aircraft and, quite frankly, this had knocked the stuffing out of the squadron morale for a considerable time to come. Why us? This third accident was due to an engine fire during a sortie over the North Sea. The crew managed to eject safely although there was a period of time, and concern, after the ejection until flares were spotted in the area where we knew the crew must have come down in the sea. It just so happened that I was airborne at the time, I was diverted to the search area and it was I who saw the first flare. I can't tell you the joy I felt when I saw the flares being fired which indicated that the crew were in their dinghies and alive. They were rescued by helicopter.

On a one-day detachment to Sola in Norway, and following a two versus two combat sortie versus Norwegian fighters, my number two hit the upraised lip of the runway on the approach to land and the right-hand undercarriage leg was pushed into the wing. The crew were unhurt and the badly damaged aircraft was repaired and recovered back to the UK about 18 months later.

On a detachment to RAF Alconbury, to fly air combat sorties with an aggressor squadron of the United States Air Force, one of the squadron aircraft crashed on the final approach to the runway when the radome (at the front of the aircraft) came open and the aircraft ceased to be a viable flying machine. The crew ejected and were safe. I was the detachment commander.

I think that readers will agree that we had had our fair share of accidents for one squadron. No. 111 Squadron, as it always has been, was a very fine and professional fighting unit throughout this adversity. It remained, until the squadron was stood down many years later, one of the finest and key squadrons in the RAF. And, finally, when I talk about the effect on the squadron from the above accidents, to keep a sense of perspective, we must never forget the appalling losses that happened in both world wars and, indeed, the accident rate in the immediate aftermath of World War II when the RAF lost more than a 1,000 aircraft around the world, in 1946, in non-combat related accidents.

My Ben Nevis Experience

I must relate my experience of climbing Ben Nevis whilst on 111 Squadron because it tells a story. A group of wing commanders had already climbed the mountain and they had managed to link in with training flights in the area by a Wessex helicopter from the Search and Rescue Flight at Leuchars. They were therefore able to be delivered to and from the bottom of the mountain before carrying out the climb. A group of four of us squadron leaders decided that we would go one better by walking to Ben Nevis before completing the climb. Due to the squadron programme, there were only a limited amount of days in which we could complete the climb or, to put it another way, we were on a fixed timescale. Our window of opportunity was in early November 1979 and by the time we set out to climb Ben Nevis we were down to only two squadron leaders, myself and Dick Northcote.

Dick and I set out from Leuchars for Ben Nevis at around ten a.m. on day one of, I think it was four, to walk the distance and complete the climb, suitably attired, and wearing bright red socks borrowed from, and identifiable with, the RAF Leuchars mountain rescue team. As we crossed the Tay Bridge into Dundee, I remember Dick suddenly saying to me that he had decided not to drink during this expedition. I was somewhat surprised, especially as I had not made any similar such decision. Anyway, we walked on and after going about 20 or so miles our thirst was getting to us and, as we passed a suitable tavern, we looked at each other and decided to go in and have a drink to quench our thirst.

Our bright red socks were immediately recognised and we were feted by the regulars who associated us with mountain rescue. When they discovered that we were in fact a pair of fighter pilots we were feted even more. To cut a long story short, a telephone call to our wives was made to convey a situation report and they, in turn, persuaded us that it was also a good idea to have a meal while at the tavern and this we did, plus a good bottle of wine. The expedition was becoming quite enjoyable, and even more so when we were further invited to join a big party that was taking place in an upstairs room. Again, we found ourselves very much the focus of attention and enjoyed a lot of free beer. By the time we departed the pub it was now close to four in the morning, as I recall. We decided that it was far too late to pitch our tent. It was a very warm November evening and so we found a friendly hay stack in a farmer's field and simply lay down and slept on the hay in our warm clothes. Sleeping was not a problem, and it had been quite a start.

We awoke at around ten that morning and set off again on our day two walk and, actually, at this stage we were more or less on schedule. Slightly dehydrated, we drank plenty of water during our walk. After covering about 16 or 17 miles, by which time we were well and truly in to the Scottish countryside, we came across a pub which seemed to be in the middle of nowhere and, funny old thing, we decided to pop in for a little refreshment. Once again, it was the red socks that attracted attention but also, we could see the locals wondering who these aliens were who had invaded their territory. We were again welcomed with open arms and spent the evening in the pub with the locals and the very friendly landlord, sampling more Scottish beer laced down by a good number of whisky chasers. The evening finished at an earlier time but, again, we did not pitch our tent. However, that was because the landlord had offered his barn as accommodation and we had gratefully accepted. Another eventful day and this was rapidly turning into a very different, but rather entertaining, experience.

On the morning of day three, Dick and I considered our progress because we had not walked as far as we would have liked on the day before. We made a decision that it was going to be very tight to achieve our aim of climbing Ben Nevis and that was our priority. Therefore, we made a change of plan. We rang our wives and proposed that they deliver us a car in the nearest town, we would buy them lunch, and then we would drive to the foot of Ben Nevis that afternoon, ready to complete the climb on day four. This, in fact is exactly what then happened. We walked the necessary miles to the town, I can't remember the name, and after lunch we drove to the foot of Ben Nevis where, and for the first time, we pitched our tent.

On day four we were up early, and it was a nice, reasonably clear day. We then completed a straight forward and successful climb of Ben Nevis. I had my expensive Pentax camera with me and, to record our achievement, some photographs were taken, or so I thought! We also each collected a stone from the summit of the mountain, as further evidence of our climb. Well, the saga was not over. After descending the mountain, we loaded up the car and drove back to Leuchars without further incident. However, I was having trouble removing the film from my camera. Therefore, I took the camera to the station photographic section and asked them if they could remove the film. The photographer came out of the dark room and reported to me that there was, in fact, no film in the camera. Well, you can imagine what our wives said, and everyone else for that matter, but at least Dick and I know that we *did* succeed in climbing Ben Nevis.

My 34th Birthday

I celebrated my 34th birthday whilst on No. 111 Squadron, yet another story that I must tell about myself, also against myself! My birthday is on the 27th of January and, on this occasion, it was a cold January day in 1979, the day after a very enjoyable Burn's Supper. Tina had planned, obviously unknown to me, a surprise birthday party for the evening. To ensure that I was out of the way during the day, she had asked my good friend, a fellow South African also on the squadron, Chris Buncher, to suggest a game of golf at St Andrews. This had been duly arranged and, in any case, we used to play golf there most weekends, if available.

On the day, I practised my swing in the garden whilst waiting for Chris to pick me up and I was beginning to wonder why he was late. He eventually arrived and provided an appropriate explanation. However, once in the car and on our way to the golf course, Chris turned to me and said, "Rick, you do realise that the golf course is closed, don't you?" I didn't! Chris had been told by Tina to keep me away from the house until at least five p.m. and this Chris did. We went to the Jigger Pub by the golf course where we also met quite a few others. Suffice to say, we had a very pleasant afternoon, a good 'pink chit'.

I was delivered back to my house at five p.m. when I invited those with me to come in and have a drink. Tina appeared on the doorstep and said, "No way, go away!" to the others, followed by, "Rick, there is a surprise party laid on for you tonight, go and lie down". Well, I missed the first two hours of the party whilst sleeping off the excesses of the afternoon, Tina had put up signs to warn everyone that I was asleep upstairs and a great party was had by all, one that I joined a little late and, by that time, very much with a second wind.

My time on No. 111 Squadron had been very eventful. There had been many memorable times but there had also been times of great sadness. The excellence of the flying, the detachments, the intercepts of Russian aircraft, the camaraderie on the squadron, all of these experiences carry special memories. A very special moment was when the squadron won the Seed Trophy, awarded to the fighter squadron that achieved the best air-to-air gunnery results over the previous year. You only win such trophies with ability, training, good engineering and excellent teamwork. I also well remember when we flew 111 sorties over a two-day period. This achievement broke records and was quite a result, especially for the engineers. These events both happened during a memorable detachment to Malta in 1978, the last detachment by an RAF fighter squadron to RAF Luqa before the RAF left the island in September 1978. On that occasion, the boss, Gil McCluney and I, together with back-seaters, Mick Mahoney and Viv, alias 'Jean Claude', Rose, flew two Phantoms to the island for the celebrations, a momentous but sad weekend, the end of an era.

CHAPTER 9
MY FIRST STAFF APPOINTMENT AND STAFF COLLEGE

After 15 years of continuous flying duties I was expecting to find myself on the ground for a few years and this is exactly what happened. In November 1980, I was posted to the Ministry of Defence in London into a squadron leader appointment associated with operational training, a job that kept me very closely connected with the front line even though I was out of the cockpit. I enjoyed the experience and I learned a lot about working in the massive Ministry of Defence (MoD) organisation, and working with government civil servants.

I had wanted to work in the MoD, partly because I would be based in London but mainly because it is the MoD that lays down the policy and I wanted to be a policy maker rather than an implementer of policy. In the job to which I had been posted I worked directly to a wing commander, Brian Entwistle, a well-respected character. Together we were responsible for decisions about resource allocation and for setting the annual tasks for the tactical weapons units at RAF Chivenor in Devon, and RAF Brawdy in Pembrokeshire, and for a number of operational conversion units (OCU), specifically for the Harrier OCU at RAF Wittering , the Jaguar OCU at RAF Lossiemouth, and the Buccaneer OCU at RAF Honington in Suffolk.

As well as my direct boss, I had some very good more senior bosses, two in particular with whom I have remained in contact ever since. They were my then two-star boss, Air Vice-Marshal John Brownlow, a well-known aviator to this day and test pilot, and a very amenable man. Now in his 80s he continues to fly and when, in recent years I was the chairman of the General Aviation Safety Council he was, for much of that time, my deputy, and someone on whom I knew that I could totally depend for good support and advice, a wise counsel. The other was Group Captain Nigel Walpole, an officer who taught me a lot, a very fine man who I have always thought should have retired as an air marshal. To this day, I regularly see Nigel and his wife, Margreet, in the RAF Club where we share a beer or two and a good yarn. Nigel is also a well-known author of a number of aviation books, and he is a great raconteur.

Whilst working in London for the first time we lived in married quarters at White Waltham, near Maidenhead. Living there really put the icing on the cake because not only was it a pleasant location but the military very much mingled with the village community and a lot of fun was had by all. I also had the use of a squash court and tennis courts almost whenever I wished. My neighbours were all good people and the social life was exceptional. I got to know some very nice pubs two of which, in particular, I remember; the Royal Oak in Paley Street and The Bell in the lovely Berkshire village of Waltham St Lawrence. Many a beer disappeared down my gullet in these establishments, usually in the company of like-minded officers such as my good friend, David Wilby. We played squash together and, together with our wives, enjoyed an excellent social life in the local area. New friends were made and there was always much laughter. Also, in 1982, the third of my children, Ian, was born in Heatherwood Hospital, Ascot.

After two years in London I was again posted, this time to attend the RAF Staff College which was then located in Bracknell, Berkshire. In 1983 I attended No. 75 Advanced Staff Course which was a year-long posting. Although I was sorry to finish the job in London, I most certainly had no regrets that I no longer had to commute daily to London. I very much enjoyed my time at staff college. The course was attended by some 90 officers, at least 30 of whom, from mainly the military, came from other foreign and commonwealth countries. The largest group on the course were from the RAF but also on the course were officers from the other services and a number of civil servants. Aspects of the course were demanding of time and brain but overall it was a satisfying experience and I learnt a lot. It tested your potential, and also your leadership capabilities. By the end it felt that not only was I a better officer for the experience but also a more informed individual. Being on a course with people who had been specially selected because of their potential for career advancement, and with people from so many different countries, there was much to learn about international affairs and cultures. It also provided plenty of opportunity for social interaction and playing sport. The staff college at Bracknell had excellent grounds and facilities and it is very sad that the place no longer exists and has been replaced by a large estate of modern houses. I have never been fitter than I was on this course and instead of lunch I used to play squash on most days. This did lead to some difficulty keeping my eyes open during afternoon lectures in the large lecture theatre. During the course we also went away, en masse, on visits to the RAF operational theatres, to see the British Army operate in Germany and the Royal Navy at sea. We also went on visits to industry and the media. The quality of presentations to the course was excellent and we enjoyed listening to top quality speakers talking to us about international, military, political and industry affairs, and more.

I remember one particular time towards the latter stages, when I and a number of other officers went on an exchange for a week to the Luftwaffe Staff College in Hamburg. We had a magnificent week in Germany but it was the final day that became one that I will never forget. The day started at the college with a champagne breakfast to say farewell to the UK contingent. We progressed from the college to the airport where we flew back to Heathrow with British Airways. The flight was very convivial and a little more champagne was partaken. We were met at Heathrow and then transported to one of the married quarters at the staff college where one of the course directing staff, Wing Commander Garth Wensley, resided. The reason we went there was to meet and welcome an officer from the Zimbabwe Air Force, Peter Bristow, a Hawk pilot who himself had attended the RAF Staff College course and who had just been released from prison where he had wrongly been detained for a lengthy period of time.

Needless to say, it was celebrations all round and more champagne. Peter Bristow himself later went to live and work in America but has since died. At four p.m. that day we all went to the college, as planned, to be told our fates/postings. I was absolutely thrilled with my posting, I was to be promoted to wing commander and become officer commanding of the new Tornado Air Defence Variant Operational Conversion Unit, a prime job and the one that I had earmarked for many years as the job that I wanted. My timing was perfect. Then it was to the bar to celebrate and then back to Garth's place where I was linking up with my wife and where the party would continue. What happened then was that my celebrations came to a very abrupt halt at seven p.m. when my wife, Tina, arrived and pulled me aside to give me the very sad news that my father had died earlier that afternoon. That ended a day that I will never ever forget, a day on which, on the one hand, I received some of the best news that I had ever received and on the other hand, also the worst news. Two days later I was back in South Africa at my mother's side, the RAF were fantastic with their support and made all the arrangements. I am just sorry that my father was unable to be told the good news about my promotion and plum posting.

After saying farewell to my father in South Africa I returned to staff college to complete my course and then, after first attending a most enjoyable Hawk refresher course at RAF Brawdy, begin the next very exciting chapter in my career and life.

One final word about my year at RAF Staff College, I must make mention of those who were a particular inspiration to me during my year of study. Firstly the commandant, Air Vice-Marshal (later Air Chief Marshal Sir Anthony) Tony Skingsley, a great all-round officer, a good man and an inspiration to all, and secondly Group Captain Graham Pitchfork (later Air Commodore), the director of my group and a very positive and highly motivated officer with unlimited energy. He was a great motivator. Graham went on, in his second career, to become a well-known author and also the aviation obituarist for the *Daily Telegraph* (to this day). A fellow student in my syndicate, Squadron Leader Mo Al-Amri, returned to Oman at the end of the course and was immediately promoted to group captain. He was destined for the very top but, unfortunately, he was killed in an aircraft accident when he was an air commodore. I did see him again before he was killed, when I led a detachment of Tornados to Masirah, Oman. He had also stayed in contact with me and, during the period when I was introducing the Tornado into RAF service, he had actually tried to persuade me to come to Oman as one of his commanders, an offer that I declined.

CHAPTER 10

INTRODUCING THE TORNADO INTO RAF SERVICE

After two tours flying the Lightning, an instructional tour on the Gnat and Hunter at RAF Valley, a Phantom tour on No. 111 Squadron at RAF Leuchars and an MoD tour looking after operational training, I felt well qualified to oversee the introduction to service of the air defence variant (ADV) of the Tornado. Indeed, to take command of the Tornado ADV Operational Conversion Unit (OCU) had been my first posting choice for several years. I had not been shy in telling people what job I wanted and, as you might well imagine, I was delighted. Thus, for me, began a long association with the Tornado, both as a squadron and station commander, in appointments at the MoD and, later, when I continued to fly the aircraft in my capacity as the Inspector of Flight Safety for the RAF.

The early days of the Tornado F2/3 were exciting times; there were many challenges and also rewards. The aircraft, on retirement in 2009, some 25 years after its introduction to service, was a very capable fighter and it had been a long road to achieve this capability. However, I like to think that right back in the early days we sowed the seeds that led to the great improvements that followed. Introducing the Tornado F2/3 into service is a story in itself and in this chapter I aim to record what happened, and to give you my own impressions from flying the aircraft, and as a part of the management chain.

Preparations for Aircraft Delivery

Preparations for the arrival of the first aircraft had been going on for several years before the actual delivery of the first two Tornado F2s on 5th November 1984. A course design team, headed up by Squadron Leader Nobby Clark, had been set up and was particularly busy throughout 1983 and 1984. At the conclusion of my advanced staff college course I refreshed on the Hawk and the Phantom and then took command of the embryo No. 229 OCU. This number plate had previously belonged to the Hunter OCU at RAF Chivenor and was the one that we sought because of its history. Throughout 1984, whilst continuing to make preparations for the arrival of the first aircraft, those of us with flying appointments on the Tornado OCU stayed current flying the Phantom with our sister OCU (No. 228) at RAF Coningsby.

During 1984 the OCU continued with a slow build-up of personnel. The course design team (Nobby Clark and Mark Micallef-Eynaud) were to become flight commanders on the OCU and the education officer on the team, Squadron Leader Ken Richardson, also joined the OCU staff. The first senior engineering officer, Squadron Leader (later AVM) David Hobart, who had talked himself into the job when I met him whilst doing my Hawk refresher course at RAF Brawdy, joined the OCU in mid-1984 and took command of the small, but highly qualified and very experienced, group of engineers who had been making the engineering preparations. This small core of engineers had mainly come from the Tornado Tri-National Training Establishment (TTTE) at RAF Cottesmore and they were absolutely invaluable to the preparations.

As already mentioned, the first aircraft were delivered to RAF Coningsby from the then British Aerospace Warton facility on 5th November 1984. The crews on these delivery flights were Mr Jerry Lee (chief test pilot) with Air Vice-Marshal Ken Hayr (Air Officer Commanding No. 11 Group) in one aircraft, and Mr Dave Eagles (executive director flight operations) and myself in the second aircraft. Formal conversion training of the first crews did not begin at Warton until January 1985 and so the first two aircraft delivered, after formal engineering acceptance, were initially used for engineering training and other preparations.

During 1984, and through into 1985 and beyond, the various ground training aids were commissioned; the cockpit emergencies and procedures trainer (CEPT), the Tornado air intercept trainer (TAIT) and the full mission simulators to name some of the training aids, and there were many other lesser training aids for use in a variety of ground school functions. The ground school was under the command of Squadron Leader Mac MacKendrick as the chief ground instructor. His ground school instructors, some of whom had been involved with preparations for several years as the project officers for specific equipment, were some of the first to join the new No. 229 OCU.

Tornado Aircraft Conversion at British Aerospace Warton

Initial conversion training for the first four crews took place on two courses at the British Aerospace airfield at Warton, in early 1985. Those on the first course, which began on 4th February 1985, were: pilots: myself and Squadron Leader Chris Stevens, and navigators: Squadron Leaders Nobby Clark and Andy Lister-Tomlinson. Those on the second course, which began a month later, were: Squadron Leader Mark Micallef-Eynaud and Flight Lieutenant Simon Manning (pilots) and Flight Lieutenants Ian Malin and Viv Rose (navigators). Our instructors at British Aerospace were all old friends from the RAF (test pilots, Peter Gordon-Johnson and Keith Hartley, and test navigators, Les Hurst and Jim Stuttard). The Tornado F2/3 was progressively to replace both the Lightning and the Phantom and hence the initial crews came primarily from the Lightning and Phantom forces. A number of aircrew joined the new OCU on return from exchange postings, and others on a return to the air-defence role after tours on the Tornado GR1. I know that it was particularly difficult for the ex-Lightning pilots to settle into what was an alien crew environment and on an aircraft which did not match the Lightning in high-level engine performance.

The courses at British Aerospace Warton involved ground school and a conversion course of just 13 sorties. This included, for pilots, general handling, a rear-seat conversion, some intercept training and air combat. On 29th March 1985, with Nobby Clark as my navigator, we flew the first all-RAF-crewed sortie to land at Coningsby, at the same time delivering the third aircraft to the RAF. Tornado F2 flying began in earnest out of Coningsby on 2nd April 1985 and, although we had only three aircraft at that stage, I flew no less than 21 sorties in that first month.

Tornado F2/Spitfire Synchronised Display

We had only been back at Coningsby for a short time when the AOC, AVM Ken Hayr, called me one evening and put the proposition to me that, as a lead-in to the 50th anniversary year of the first flight of the Spitfire in March 1986, it would be nice to do a synchronised display depicting the old (Spitfire) and the new (Tornado F2). He received an immediate positive and enthusiastic response from me, after which discussions began in earnest with the Battle of Britain Memorial Flight about the detail of the display.

There were, at that stage, only two pilots at Coningsby qualified to fly the

Tornado, myself and Chris Stevens. Chris had had an unfortunate bicycle accident which resulted in concussion, and to him being grounded for some time. This, of course, meant that there was now only one pilot and that is how I came to be involved in what turned out to be a highly enjoyable and much acclaimed display throughout the 1985 display season.

The Tornado is an easy aircraft to fly and, to the surprise of others, it was very comfortable to operate in formation with the Spitfire at 175 knots. The synchronisation of the display relied on the radio transmissions of the Spitfire and the ability of the Tornado to make rapid speed adjustments. It was a very successful display season helped significantly by the professionalism of Squadron Leader Paul Day (the Major) in the Spitfire. It is also a testament to the flying qualities of the Tornado that I felt totally comfortable about becoming involved in this display less than six weeks after I had started my conversion to the aircraft. Rear-seat aircrew who flew with me during displays in 1985 were Group Captain Mike Elsam (station commander Coningsby), and Squadron Leaders Andy Lister-Tomlinson and Nobby Clark; it was all a memorable opportunity, and display, which I still find is talked about to this day.

No. 229 OCU Build-Up and No. 65 Squadron Operational Work-Up

After our return from aircraft conversion at BAE Warton the work-up of No. 229 OCU gathered pace. Initially, we consolidated our training on the aircraft and validated the various syllabi that had been put together by the course design team. We also had to ratify instructor qualifications and work ourselves up to be ready to teach the first of two instructor courses which began in the autumn of 1985.

The official reformation of No. 229 OCU took place on 8th July 1985. The conversion and work-up of the OCU instructors, and, as I recall, there were about eight crews per course, went on well into 1986. I had had a lot of input into the selection of the first instructor crews when I was invited to visit the Headquarters for Personnel and asked to indicate which pilots and navigators I would like selected to join my staff. This included a number of ex-Phantom air defenders who had been flying and instructing on the Tornado GR1 at either RAF Cottesmore or RAF Honington. The OCU was also working up to be ready for declaration to NATO, as No. 65 (F) Squadron, on 31st December 1986. I had sought the No. 65 Squadron number plate because it was a Battle of Britain squadron with a proud history and I had also been a member of No. 65 Squadron whilst flying Lightnings at RAF Coltishall. A decision had been taken, because of delays in the build-up of Tornado F3 squadrons, that it was necessary to appoint the OCU (No. 65 Squadron) as the first Tornado F3 squadron to be declared to NATO in order to meet RAF commitments. This put added demands on all areas of the OCU and it is a great credit to all those involved that all targets were met or exceeded, and on time. The OCU was fully prepared by the time the first squadron course began at the beginning of 1987.

There were many challenges to be met and clearances to be achieved in those initial months. All instructors, after aircraft conversion, then had to go through instructor conversion and a full operational work-up programme. In May 1986, we carried out air-combat training at the air combat manoeuvring installation (ACMI) range in Decimomannu in Sardinia. In November 1986, we deployed to Cyprus to carry out the first Tornado armament practice camp. This not only proved our deployment capability but, also, our air-to-air gun firing results were such that No. 229 OCU/65 Squadron won the prestigious Seed Trophy, awarded to the top-scoring fighter squadron in No. 11 Group at air-to-air gunnery. This was an excellent achievement at the very first attempt. In October 1986, we carried out a missile practice camp at RAF Valley where I had the privilege of undertaking the first in-service Tornado F2/3 firing of a Skyflash missile; it hit the target. Throughout all these efforts the engineering staff, in particular, were quite outstanding. For example, not seen publicly were the extreme efforts by the engineers to carry out work associated with equipment clearances before we could fire the weapons. Everything was new and we were paving the way for the future.

The first 18 aircraft to be delivered to the RAF were all Tornado F2s but no sooner had we received the last F2 than we then began the task of replacing these aircraft with the more capable F3s. There were many differences between the two aircraft, most of which were associated with the aircraft systems. Perhaps the biggest changes were an increased main computer capacity (from 64 KB to 128 KB), a digital engine control unit (DECU) to replace the mechanical engine control unit (MECU), and an increase in engine power. The most noticeable external clue to the mark of Tornado was the fact that the F3 had an extended jet pipe. The first RAF F3 sortie took place on 6th August 1986 (crew: Wing Commander Rick Peacock-Edwards and Group Captain Mike Elsam). By the time No. 229 OCU was declared to NATO as No. 65 (Fighter) Squadron the unit had over 20 aircraft, over 40 aircrew and approaching 300 engineering and support staff; it had grown into a very large unit.

Problem Areas/Issues

Radar

The radar had been a problem area since the start and we had our first look at the nature of the situation during our conversion flying at Warton. The major problem was associated with spurious blips (targets). At times there were so many spurious blips on the radar screen that it was almost impossible to identify the real target. The situation did improve as newer marks of the radar were introduced but major action was necessary if we were to achieve the deadline for operational declaration. We had kept the various staffs well informed of our concerns and eventually a major meeting took place at Head-quarters Strike Command to discuss the issue and agree a way ahead. This resulted in a trial, Trial Bunbury, to analyse the radar problems; this trial led to a costly series of emergency modifications and was an important milestone for the aircraft and its future.

A lot has been said over the years about the time when there were insuffi-cient radars to fit into all aircraft, and a limited number of aircraft had cement fitted in the nose in place of the radar; hence the term 'Blue Circle Radar'. However, as I have said, only a few aircraft (about six as I recall) did not have radars fitted and then only for a short period of time in early 1986. The reason for the lack of radars was because of the need to modify existing radars back at GEC; in short, the planned delivery schedule had to be amended, hence the temporary lack of radars.

Aircraft Fatigue

When we first started operating the Tornado F2 we had no fatigue formulae available, as I recall, but we were told that fatigue was not expected to be a problem and so we pulled 'g' with great freedom. However, as the formulae became available, it became clear that we did indeed have a problem. This resulted in some rapid changes in the way we operated in order to help con-serve aircraft fatigue. Later, however, we were told that the fatigue formulae were in fact wrong and that, after all, the problems were in fact not so great. This was good news, to put it mildly. Suffice to say that in the early days there was considerable confusion over the subject of aircraft fatigue.

The Engine

The engine was not a major problem other than it ran out of puff in the medium to higher levels (at subsonic speeds), an operational limitation. It had been very much designed for low-level operations in the Tornado GR1. It was superb at low level.

Notable Events and Achievements during the Introduction to Service Phase

Flypasts

On 14th June 1986, when we only had a total complement of 10 aircraft, we flew a nine-aircraft formation flypast over Buckingham Palace in honour of the Queen's 60th birthday. It was a perfect day for it, clear and blue. On our return to Coningsby we opened the Families Day that had been planned to coincide with the Buckingham Palace event with another flypast. Five aircraft from the formation then landed at Coningsby whilst I led four aircraft in a rendezvous with a tanker aircraft out over the North Sea. After taking on fuel we then returned to Coningsby where I led a four-aircraft formation display before landing. What a day! Also, in 1986 (24th July), I led the flypast to mark the opening of the Commonwealth Games in Edinburgh. I well remember that flypast and the BBC trying to influence (through me) a change in the timing of the flypast to create surprise. Needless to say, I did not listen! On 22nd May 1986 I led a composite 16-aircraft flypast of No. 11 (Fighter) Group over Mildenhall (Tornado F2s/Lightnings/Phantoms and Hawks) prior to the Mildenhall Air Display; this was the only time that these aircraft were ever to fly in formation together; it was, therefore, a unique 'fighter' event. I also led two flypasts for the Queen Mother, one over the RAF Museum at Hendon, London and the other over the Joint Services Staff College at Greenwich, London.

Exercise Saif Sareea 1986

In November 1986, No. 229 OCU took part in Exercise Saif Sareea 1 in Oman. This involved a ten-and-a-half-hour deployment flight, mainly over-night, from RAF Coningsby to Masirah in Oman where we had to arrive at exactly nine thirty a.m. in front of many VVIPs; we arrived to the second, much to the pleasure of the then commander-in-chief Strike Command, Air

Chief Marshal Sir Peter Harding. In the eyes of the world, this deployment demonstrated the RAF's global reach capability and it was a key milestone in the introduction phase of the Tornado F2/3. Over the next few weeks No. 229 played a full and successful part in the exercise.

Defence Sales Support

Also, in November 1986, at the conclusion of the Oman deployment, No. 229 OCU visited Jordan where we had the honour of being hosted by King Hussain. He attended briefings, hosted us at lunch and listened to the debriefs after we had flown senior pilots from the Royal Jordanian Air Force. In March 1987, I led a detachment of two F3s on a defence sales tour of the Middle East. We visited Bahrain, Qatar, and the UAE.

What was it Like to Fly the Tornado F2/3?

Personally, I find this a very easy question to answer; it was a pure delight. A lot of hard work had been put into the design of the aircraft and it paid off. The aircraft controls were well harmonised, the cockpit environment was, without question, the best that I had encountered; it was quiet and easy to manage. At low level the Tornado simply rode through all that the elements could throw at you, and the aircraft gave a very smooth ride at all times. It was a joy to fly throughout the speed range, from 150 knots right up to the maximum speed of Mach 2.0 or 800 knots at low level. The low-level performance, in particular, was very impressive and you could accelerate from 250 knots to over 600 knots in significantly less than 30 seconds. Finally, the aircraft handled well and the controls were lighter (30%) than its sister aircraft, the then Tornado GR1. This gave it more of a 'fighter feel'.

It was also a great comfort to fly an aircraft where back-up systems had been carefully considered. To this end, the quadruplex fly-by-wire flying control system was perhaps the best example; there was plenty of redundancy and if all else failed, which it never did, you still had a mechanical back-up system to enable you safely to recover the aircraft to base. Similarly, I found the innovative spin prevention and incidence limiting system (SPILS) a great comfort to fly with because you knew that it was protecting you from getting yourself into some potentially nasty situations and it did enable 'carefree handling'.

I found the wing-sweeping capability an interesting novelty but the system worked admirably and it was simple to operate. The ability to sweep the wings to a number of positions certainly added a lot of flexibility to operations. You swept them to various positions dependant on speed but if you had the wings in the wrong position then the aircraft, mainly through a little mild vibration/buffet, tended to remind you to move the levers, i.e. sweep the wings to a different position. The F3 was planned to be fitted with an auto wing-sweep capability and I was involved in meetings associated with the introduction of this development. In the end, I was sorry to see that this was not introduced because the development of the system had gone well (as I recall) but I believe that it was mainly cost that prevented this happening. I can't honestly say that we weren't coping quite adequately without the auto wing-sweep facility and so, in all probability, it would have been more of a luxury than a necessity.

I have already made mention of the problems that we had with the radar in the initial days; suffice to say, again, that the radar capability at the end of the in-service life of the aircraft bears little resemblance to that at the beginning, such has been the (impressive) development of the system. It was also a great joy to operate a radar with a multi-track-while-scan capability, at the time of introduction a major advance in RAF operational fighter capability. The 'TVs' fitted in the cockpits were excellent and the ability to switch modes, as required in individual cockpits, was very useful. The Tornado F2/3 took 'fighter' navigation and situational awareness to a new level and it was very comforting to have so much capability available.

I do remember the way in which the aircraft was advertised before it came into service, quote: 'A fighter equipped with advance medium-range air-to-air missiles (AMRAAM) and advance short-range air-to-air missiles (ASRAAM), and joint tactical information distribution system (JTIDS) etc.'. Personally, I found it a great disappointment that the reality was very different and that these capabilities, with the notable exception of JTIDS, were still some years away from introduction. By the time that the aircraft went out of service in 2010, and this fact is very typical of other mature operational RAF aircraft in the past, the full capability of the Tornado F3 and its systems had been more than proven. I would argue, in particular, that the significant weapon capability, coupled with the JTIDS facility, has taken the development of RAF fighter tactics to new levels.

The communication systems were also vastly improved, with access to both UHF and VHF, an HF radio, a secure 'Havequick' radio capability, and the ability to record and play tapes, so important for the debriefs. In general, there were greatly increased developments over previous fighter aircraft. The systems in the Tornado F2/3 were a significant leap forward and the aircraft was 'user friendly'. The operating environment was very conducive to good crew co-operation, and the best crews were those that worked best together. The role of the navigator had disappeared and the 'navigator' was now very much a 'weapon systems operator' (WSO).

So what were the downsides in those early days? Well, I have already mentioned the problems that we had with the radar, also the limitations of the engines at the medium to higher levels; apart from these I think the only major downside was the time taken to introduce the more capable AMRAAM and ASRAAM systems and, to a lesser extent, the JTIDS capability.

However, and perhaps not necessarily totally associated with the early introduction to service, a few words about the relationship with industry. I saw this over a number of tours associated with the Tornado, at station level and whilst at the Ministry of Defence (MoD) in a variety of staff appointments; there were big differences in perspective. During my involvement with industry from a station level perspective, both as a squadron and later station commander, I always felt that the relationship with industry was excellent, and I cannot praise enough the welcome and help that we were given during our initial conversion to the aircraft at British Aerospace Warton, and in our dealings with other companies. On the other hand, whilst serving in MoD staff appointments, I became both frustrated and, to an extent, disillusioned by the confrontational approach that I witnessed at some of the meetings that I attended, in particular, at some of those between the then MoD procurement executive and industry. A situation where both sides used to spend too much time blaming each other for a variety of failures, and a general unwillingness to compromise, invariably resulted in no, or even negative, progress. On these occasions, and I hasten to add that it was by no means at all meetings, I remember thinking at the time how poorly both sides used to conduct themselves, often using tactics that, quite frankly, were never helpful to anyone. Of course, I am talking about the situation as it was over 25 years ago and I presume that the working relationship between the MoD and industry is now much more harmonious, or is it?

The fact that the Tornado was a multi-nation aircraft (UK, Germany and Italy) had both pluses and minuses. Interoperability was a plus but a downside was the time taken to staff such things as modifications through the multi-national headquarters in Munich. The UK was the only one of the original three nations initially to procure the F2/3 but, in the main, we still had to accord with the multi-national control, and this often resulted in delays associated with decision making and change, and, ultimately, this involved time.

The People

It would be wrong of me to write this chapter without making mention of the people involved with the Tornado F2/3, and I know that the same can also be said for other aircraft and systems. I will not single out specific individuals for praise, quite frankly there are too many who deserve to be acclaimed. In short, I will always remember the excellence of the people involved, and the flexibility of thought, the initiative, the willingness to work hard and, most importantly, the sheer ability and quality of all personnel, be they engineers or aircrew, educators or administrative staff. The RAF has always provided the very best training and this has provided great dividends from an operational perspective. It is one of the key reasons why the RAF is such a respected service, and why it is, quite frankly, the best. I was proud to serve with such excellent people, also to have my own personal experience of such high training standards, and to have led people of such quality.

The above pages are by no means an extensive report of those early Tornado F2/3 days, or of the life of the aircraft. However, I hope that they have given a snapshot of how the aircraft was introduced into service, an insight into some of the activities that took place, a glimpse of what the aircraft was like to fly, and also some of the behind-the-scenes activities. My involvement with the Tornado F2/3 has provided me with many memorable experiences. Much was achieved during the 25 years that the aircraft was in-service. How quickly have the years passed for it seems only a short time ago that I was the first RAF pilot to convert to the aircraft at British Aerospace Warton.

At the end of my fantastic and challenging tour to introduce the Tornado F2/3 into RAF service I was awarded the Air Force Cross (AFC) and also a very prestigious prize, the Arthur Barrett Memorial Prize. I did see the citation for that prize which made me feel ten feet tall, which I reprint below not because I wish to grab attention but because it provides a record for historical purposes.

'The Arthur Barrett Memorial Prize for 1986 has been awarded to Wing Commander R S Peacock-Edwards, OC No. 229 OCU, RAF Coningsby, in recognition of his outstanding skill and leadership in the air, and his major personal contribution to the operational development and introduction into service of the Tornado F2/F3.

'Wing Commander Peacock-Edwards, a general duties pilot and qualified flying instructor, served as Officer Commanding No. 229

Operational Conversion Unit from October 1984 until June 1987.

'From the introduction into service of the Tornado F2/F3 until he relinquished command, Wing Commander Peacock-Edwards played a significant part in the development of the aircraft, both operationally and from a public relations standpoint. He was the first RAF officer to be converted to this type of aircraft, and he was also personally involved in creating plans for its tactical employment. Additionally, he demonstrated the aircraft to the public throughout the 1985 season, flying a synchronised display with a Spitfire at several major air shows.

'In 1986 he relinquished the routine display role to concentrate on the task of introducing the aircraft into operational service. Nevertheless, he continued to lead formation displays, and in May 1986 he flew as the leader of a mixed fighter formation at the Mildenhall Air Show. The formation consisted of 16 aircraft, drawn from each of the fighter squadrons in No. 11 Group, and it was a truly unique occasion. The following month, he led his squadron in a diamond nine formation over Buckingham Palace as the RAF contribution to Her Majesty the Queen's official birthday celebrations; these aircraft subsequently carried out a display for the public at an open day on their return to RAF Coningsby. In July 1986, he led a formation flypast over the reception at the RAF Museum at Hendon, attended by Her Majesty Queen Elizabeth, the Queen Mother, to mark the 50th anniversary of the formation of the RAF's functional commands. Later the same month, he was the formation leader of four Tornado F3s and four Phantoms to mark the opening of the Commonwealth Games, at the Meadowbank Stadium in Edinburgh; these tasks were all carried out with characteristic precision and professionalism.

'Wing Commander Peacock-Edwards has also done much to promote the virtues of the Tornado to potential overseas buyers, having on many occasions demonstrated the aircraft to foreign dignitaries and influential representatives from the aviation press. This aspect of his performance in the air is particularly noteworthy and culminated in his outstanding efforts in leading the Air Defence contingent on Exercise Saif Sareea, a very successful deployment to Oman in November 1986. The aim of this tri-service exercise was to demonstrate the UK's capability for out of area operations and to practise combined operations with the Sultan of Oman's Armed Forces. In the event, the Tornado F3 aircraft flew direct to Masirah from the UK, a journey of over ten hours duration, using a Tristar K1 for tanker support. Senior Omanis as well as the Secretary of State for Defence, and many senior representatives of the press and media were present when the aircraft arrived precisely on schedule, so demonstrating most effectively both the capabilities of the Tornado and the feasibility of rapid long-range deployments from the UK.

'As an adjunct to the exercise the aircraft took part in Exercise Buhl in Jordan from 2nd to 4th December 1986 during which senior members of the Jordanian Air Force were given an opportunity to fly in the Tornado F3. Once again, Wing Commander Peacock-Edwards used his personal flying skills to demonstrate the aircraft to good effect, earning praise from Headquarters No. 11 Group for his outstanding leadership and performance in the air.

'His success in leading No. 229 Operational Conversion Unit towards its declaration as No. 65 (Reserve) Squadron has been no less impressive. His unit completed a highly successful missile practice camp at RAF Valley in October 1986, and he fired the first live Skyflash missile from a Tornado during the detachment. Similarly, his unit carried out a very satisfactory armament practice camp in Cyprus, and produced the best air-to-air gunnery results from a RAF air defence squadron for many years. During each of these detachments Wing Commander Peacock-Edwards set an outstanding example both on the ground and in the air, and it is very much to his personal credit that No. 65 (Reserve) Squadron was declared to NATO as our first operational Tornado F2/F3 unit on time on 31st December 1986.'

CHAPTER 11
TORNADO LEADER

After handing over command of No. 65 Squadron/229 OCU at RAF Coningsby, it was not surprising that my next three appointments all carried responsibility for the Tornado F3. In June 1987 I was posted to the Ministry of Defence in London to take charge of the Tornado role. I had wanted to return to the MoD to be involved in the policy side of the business and I also enjoyed London. I was in this appointment for 18 months, a busy period that covered the continued build-up of the Tornado squadrons in place of those of the Lightning and Phantom. As always there were many issues to deal with and it was a demanding job. My time in this post also carried frustrations which I had not previously appreciated.

I regularly used to attend tri-national meetings in Munich related to aircraft modifications. Although at the time the UK was the only nation to be operating the air defence variant of the Tornado, as stated previously many of the modifications in the pipeline still needed tri-nation approval. I found this a burdensome and time-wasting process. It also seemed to overall increase costs. Whilst I am well aware of some of the benefits of multi-national programmes, I also began to learn about some of the difficulties to be overcome.

I also saw another side of relations with industry. Whilst flying the aircraft at Coningsby there had been a superb relationship with industry and I expected this to continue in my London job. However, this was not the case. I used to attend meetings between the MoD procurement executive and British Aerospace to discuss programme development matters and I was appalled from the outset by the confrontational attitude of both sides (see also page 119). I have always strongly believed that the way to do business is to work together towards a common aim but some of these meetings used to result in absolutely zero achievement. The experience taught me a lot about how, in my view, not to do business, I learnt a lot. To this end, I have in the 30 years since these experiences seen a vast improvement in inter-organisation relationships, to the benefit of all. There is also evident a much greater degree of all-round professionalism.

During this tour I also found myself involved in several joint MoD/British Aerospace trips to Saudi Arabia in support of work associated with defence exports. The Saudis had decided to procure the Tornado F3 during my time at Coningsby commanding the operational conversion unit, an almost unexpected decision from the speed of decision-making factor but a very welcome decision for both the UK government and industry. I like to think that I played my part in the Saudi decision to procure 24 Tornado F3s and I believe that I did. I certainly enjoyed my involvement with British Aerospace on these visits and the associated work. Our relationship was again excellent and so different from what I had seen at other meetings in London. I also went on another Tornado F3 defence sales mission to Kuala Lumpur, a visit that I, again, greatly enjoyed. I know that a move was made to see if I could return to Malaysia to take over from the incumbent RAF representative dealing with the Malaysian authorities, a good friend, Mike Rudd, who was due to return to the UK. However, I also became aware in the process that the RAF had other plans for my future and so it did not happen.

At the end of 1989 I was promoted to group captain and took over from my then boss in the MoD, John May, as deputy director of Air Defence. In this post, as well as overseeing the Tornado F3, I had a much wider remit and responsibility for all other air-defence aircraft and weapons and also for surface-to-air missiles operated by the RAF Regiment. I had a really good team working for me and, in turn, I reported to the director of Air Defence, Air Commodore Ian McBride, a fellow Lightning pilot who to this day remains a good friend. A clever man, I always liked his "management by perambulation" (his words) style. I very much enjoyed working with him as a team and we oversaw a number of important changes during my time in the post. It was during this appointment that I also got to know NATO better and I regularly travelled to Brussels to attend meetings. This in itself was an interesting diversion from my other responsibilities and I used to enjoy my visits, usually accompanied by Wing Commander Dave Kuun, another fellow Lightning pilot who, like me, had originally come into the RAF from South Africa.

Whilst I was in the post, I also had responsibility for progressing the introduction of air-combat training using an air-combat manoeuvring installation located in a large area in the North Sea off the coast of East Anglia. I worked closely with British Aerospace and others to bring on line this capability and I remember becoming very frustrated with the lack of progress, mainly due to funding complications within the MoD. In fact, I was so frustrated that I eventually came to an interim agreement with the British Aerospace project officer to commence the important training which was so necessary. I won't go into detail but suffice to say that I found myself in a degree of trouble about what I had done, mainly with civil servants, and I had some explaining to do, but I survived this little bit of difficulty. This all happened in January 1990 during my last week in post as deputy director Air Defence, and it certainly made that last week in post exciting. So, after what had been another short one-year tour of duty I moved on to my next challenge as station commander of RAF Leeming in Yorkshire.

Station Commander RAF Leeming

I had had good warning that I was being considered for a station commander appointment when, about eight to nine months before I left the MoD, I had been contacted to ask that if I was to be given a command appointment would I intend to do so accompanied. I had replied in the affirmative and some months later heard the good news that I was to take command of RAF Leeming in June 1990. Prior to taking up the appointment I had to attend a number of briefings from various RAF departments and also complete a short Tornado refresher course at the same unit that I had commanded just over two years earlier. All went according to plan and in the last week of June 1990 I arrived at RAF Leeming to take over from my predecessor, Group Captain John Rooum. John and I had known each other for many years having both flown Lightnings briefly together on No. 92 Squadron. John had also been group captain operations at Headquarters No. 11 Group whilst I had been introducing the Tornado F2/3 into RAF service. Our handover was to last a week and, on the Friday, John and I had a formal handover, he and his wife departed the station commander's residence and my wife arrived laden with children, dog, cats and hamsters to begin our next adventure.

Leeming was one of the fighter bases within No. 11 Group, headquartered at RAF Bentley Priory, the alma mater of fighter pilots. I reported to the Air Officer Commanding who was, initially, Air Vice-Marshal Bill Wratten (later Air Chief Marshal Sir William) and then Air Vice-Marshal John Allison (later Air Chief Marshal Sir John). I was always appreciative of the way in which they allowed me to run my station with minimal interference. The senior air staff officer at No. 11 Group was Air Commodore (later Air Vice-Marshal) Mike Donaldson. He and I used to play a lot of squash together and were also both to become, in turn, president of RAF Squash.

Leeming was a big base and, at the time, the most modern in the RAF. This was because during the 1980s it had been closed for several years to allow a re-build of facilities in preparation for the arrival of the Tornados. NATO and MoD funding provided excellent new facilities to better enable the airfield to maintain operations in even the most extreme war situations. These included hardened aircraft shelters and other hardened facilities. A new air traffic control tower was also built. The airfield was sited close to the main A1 highway which runs from London through to Scotland and a new bridge was built over the motorway to better allow access to the station via a new road to the base. Leeming was one of the most important front-line airfields in the UK. Based there were three Tornado squadrons (Nos. 11, 23 and 25 Squadrons), an RAF Regiment squadron (No. 15, later to re-number to No. 54 Squadron), the Northumbrian Universities Air Squadron, an air experience flight, and a mountain rescue team. There were around 2,000 mainly serving personnel on base and with dependants we had a community of over 5,000. It was a great challenge and one that I absolutely relished. I already knew all the senior staff but there were many new faces and friends to make.

Little more than one month after taking command Saddam Hussein invaded Kuwait, on 2nd August 1990, and the situation developed apace. We knew that the government was considering sending fighters to the Gulf and the order was made to do so on 7th August. This decision was to change my life for the next few months.

The Gulf Crisis 1990-1991

Much has been written about the Gulf War in 1991 but little has been said about the overall build-up to that war and in particular the initial response to the situation that arose after Iraq invaded Kuwait on 2nd August 1990. My personal involvement in the build-up was both exciting and interesting, because it was a real situation and a great test of leadership and decision making. I and my team found ourselves in a demanding situation where urgency was a key word.

Events moved quickly after the initial invasion and there was constant dialogue between the US and her closest ally, the UK. The invasion itself had caught the world by surprise and there was a need to move fast, not just because Kuwait had been invaded but also because there was concern that Iraq could move into Saudi Arabia and onwards. The US and UK both have considerable interests in Saudi Arabia and of course there was the oil factor. The decision to deploy forces to Saudi Arabia was rapidly made by the respective governments and began without delay.

As already stated, I was aware that the UK government was considering sending fighters to the Gulf but I did not expect personal events to evolve as quickly as they did. I was flying one afternoon when I was recalled to base. I was briefed that a decision had been taken to send fighters to the Gulf but that they were to be the two squadrons of Tornado fighters that were on exercise in the Mediterranean at that time, and based in Cyprus. These were not from my base but were the nearest to the region. I was told that consideration was being given as to who should take overall command of the UK forces.

Overnight, missiles were prepared by my weapons experts and made ready for shipment (by air) to the Gulf. The next morning, at about ten a.m., Air Marshal Dick Johns (later Air Chief Marshal Sir Richard and also chief of the Air Staff) who was at the time the senior air staff officer at Headquarters RAF Strike Command (the operational headquarters of the RAF front line) called me and told me that I was the chosen man to command the forces being deployed and that I should make my way south to the headquarters for a briefing from the commander-in-chief (C-in-C, Air Chief Marshal Sir Patrick Hine) that afternoon. One hour later I had been picked up by an executive jet and was on my way to London. I had just enough time to say farewell to my family, be issued with a weapon (gun), change into battle dress during which time I also had a doctor sticking needles into my thighs, I knew not what – and I was gone, I knew not to where until I saw the C-in-C that afternoon.

On arrival at Strike Command I was given an intelligence briefing, my security clearance was raised to a high level, and more, and later that afternoon I was briefed by the C-in-C on his return from a cabinet meeting. I was to lead the British forces deploying to Dhahran, Saudi Arabia. A team of highly skilled specialists had already been assembled at another RAF base and were awaiting my arrival and to be briefed on plans. Sir Patrick's brief to me as leader was music to my ears. He said: "Rick, you know what has happened. I don't know what situation you will find when you get to the Gulf. You are in charge, assess the situation and report back as soon as possible." I needed no more briefing; the problem was mine and I relished the prospect.

The flight out to Saudi Arabia was by Hercules aircraft. It was a long flight, which gave me time to monitor the developing situation in the Middle East, to meet with the various specialists in my team and to plan a course of action on arrival. We refuelled en route in Cyprus where I briefed the squadron commanders of the two Tornado squadrons being deployed to Saudi Arabia a mere 24 hours after my own arrival.

We arrived in Dhahran late at night and were met by officials from the UK

Ministry of Defence in the region and the senior representatives from British Aerospace (BAe) who had a significant presence in Saudi Arabia. They had done a magnificent job of preparing for our arrival. I must single out Paul Kelly, who was in charge of British Aerospace at Dhahran and the then Wing Commander Graham Bowerman (later Group Captain) who was the MoD representative in Dhahran, for their very considerable involvement and contribution to our welfare in Saudi Arabia. They were both magnificent.

The next month was probably the most challenging of my life. We had a huge amount of work to do to prepare ourselves for, initially, a possible Iraqi invasion into Saudi Arabia and then, as our numbers in theatre increased by the hour, to build up our capability to remove the Iraqis from Kuwait. Those initial days were tense and hot (52°C) and there was little sleep. There was so much to do and so little time to do it. US forces had arrived at about the same time as the British and, together with the Saudis, we all worked closely together. The base commander at Dhahran was a Saudi prince whom I had met previously when he was being trained by the RAF to fly the Lightning. To see the might of America was awesome and if I ever had any doubts about their superpower status, the sight of giant military transport aircraft, and 747s commandeered from the airlines, arriving every 15-20 minutes, day and night, answered the question. It was hugely impressive.

After arriving at Dhahran, the situation developed quickly and it was only a few days before, following further orders to send an increasing number of RAF squadrons and personnel to the Gulf, the next decision was made to send an air vice-marshal to Saudi Arabia to take overall command of RAF forces in the Gulf. I, therefore, handed over command of all British forces to the then Air Vice-Marshal Sandy Wilson (later Air Chief Marshal Sir Andrew). I then became his air defence commander and commander of the British forces at Dhahran. In this capacity, I was also given a personal SAS bodyguard for protection because the terrorist threat was assessed to be very high and I was a key target. Interestingly, I also had a 'political advisor', but I won't say what his role was in life. No-one else even knew that he was there. Sometimes I flew the Tornado fighter on air-defence patrols near the Kuwait/Iraq border although I was not personally allowed to do more than token flying because of my role as a commander on the ground. However, it was important that I was aware of what my aircrews were doing and for them to see me in the air increased my own credibility in their eyes.

For the first few weeks of my time in Dhahran the Tornados were initially under the command of Wing Commanders Euan Black and Roy Trotter before

I put the force under single command. The initial aircraft were fairly quickly replaced by modified Tornado F3s, and aircrew from the three squadrons at Leeming replaced those from Coningsby. Wing Commander Dave Hamilton, who was the boss of No. 11 Squadron at Leeming, commanded the composite wing. The replacement aircraft had had a number of modifications embodied to better suit the hot theatre of operations in the Gulf. Similarly, the replacement aircrew had completed Gulf work-up training in the UK before deployment.

To be involved in the build-up, and to see the motivation and achievement of those under my command, was a privilege that I will always remember. We built our own headquarters, we had to work hard to get permissions from the Saudis, my men and women toiled for long hours in heat that none of us had ever before experienced, and often in other very adverse conditions. Operational preparations were fast and furious and within a short time we were all talking of 'when' we were going to be required to do things, a sure sign of our increasing confidence and readiness. However, that was a mainly political decision and by the time of the war, I was back in command of Leeming. I missed the war itself but believe me I had plenty of excitement in the initial preparation phase.

I will finish by saying a few words about two other aspects of the operation, namely the role of the media and preparations for possible nuclear, biological and chemical (NBC) warfare.

I had been well trained in how to deal with the media because it was something that I had dealt with on a daily basis back in the UK but I was certainly not prepared for the scale of the media attention on this occasion. There were literally hundreds of press based on my doorstep in Dhahran requesting interviews, asking questions and looking for stories. Fortunately, I had a public relations officer on my staff, himself a professional journalist, so he was able to control my involvement. My first PR officer was Gerry Monte and he was replaced after a few months by Keith Skues, of BBC Radio 1 fame. They both held commissions in the RAF Volunteer Reserve and were members of a Volunteer Reserve PR Flight. Their contribution was vital and they were an essential part of my team. I became friends with household names from the various international TV news companies (such as CNN, Sky, BBC and ITV). I adopted the principle that I recognised they (the media) had a job to do and they, in turn, should recognise that I too had a major task on my hands. It worked and I had an excellent relationship with the media but I made the effort, and it was very worthwhile.

Turning to NBC operations, this is a most complex and serious business and preparing to defend oneself against a nuclear, biological or chemical threat requires knowledge and extensive training. It is not comfortable. We had special clothing to wear and special breathing apparatus in the cockpits of our aircraft. We looked like men from outer space in our NBC suits and there was a real inconvenience having to wear them in such high temperatures. This was the one area where I had disagreements with some of those back in the temperate UK climate who clearly had little idea of the problems associated with operating in the very high temperatures in the Gulf. I made in theatre decisions about our operating policy and, in this matter, I was given the full support of the commander-in-chief during his not infrequent visits to the Gulf. I really appreciated his support, at all times.

Return to Leeming

In October 1990 I handed over as the UK air defence commander at Dhahran to Group Captain John Rooum from whom, of course, only a few months earlier I had taken over command of RAF Leeming. At that time, we certainly had no idea of the events that were to follow. Exciting times! I returned to the UK on board an RAF Hercules aircraft ready to resume my command of Leeming. In my absence, my deputy, Group Captain Kip Smith, had done an admirable job as the acting station commander as, I must add, had my wife Tina, in her role as wife of the station commander. In fact, it is worth recording here the great support that she gave me throughout my time in command, as had been the case on all of my previous tours, and would continue to be the case on future tours. The contribution of the wives to service life and welfare can be immense and they all deserve great credit for the role that they play.

To some extent it felt strange returning from the heat of the desert to autumn in the UK but I was quickly back in the thick of things at Leeming. A number of aircrew and engineers were already deployed to Saudi Arabia under the No. 11 (Fighter) Squadron number plate although in fact the personnel had been selected from all three Tornado F3 squadrons based at Leeming. Most returned at the end of the year. For me, the fact that I had been in Saudi Arabia and was very familiar with the situation and environment, meant that I was in a good position to talk about developments and, in particular, to help reassure the families.

The First Gulf War itself followed early in 1991 and was quickly over. By the spring of 1991 all was returning to normal at Leeming and that remained the case for the rest of my tour as station commander. There were many challenges and my time was fully occupied. There were the usual number of exercises to keep everyone operationally on their toes and we also had to prepare for a full Taceval of the station which successfully took place in early 1992. However, it was also the start of a time of change for the RAF in general. The Cold War was now over and we progressively became focused on the new emerging world.

I used to fly the Tornado two or three times per week, alternating between squadrons, and on Friday afternoons I would fly the Bulldogs belonging to Northumbrian University Air Squadron. I thoroughly enjoyed my Friday afternoon flying in an aircraft from which I could better survey my parish and the local area. It also used to set me up nicely for the Friday evening happy hour.

My squadron commanders at Leeming were all old friends. Wing Commander (later Group Captain) David Hamilton, an ex-Lightning pilot and who had also flown Phantoms on HMS *Ark Royal* while on secondment to the Royal Navy, commanded No. 11 Squadron and, on posting, he was replaced by Wing Commander (later Air Vice-Marshal) John Cliffe, another ex-Lightning pilot. No. 23 Squadron was initially commanded by Wing Commander (later Air Commodore) Neil Taylor, an ex-Phantom pilot and then by Wing Commander (later Air Commodore) Andy Lambert, an ex-Phantom 'fightergator'. No. 25 Squadron was led initially by Wing Commander Mick Martin, an ex-Phantom 'fightergator', and then by Wing Commander (later Group Captain) John Middleton, also an ex-Phantom 'fightergator'. The officer commanding Operations Wing was initially Group Captain Kip Smith and he was succeeded by Wing Commander Sandy Davis, an ex-Lightning pilot and old friend from both my Gütersloh and Coltishall days. The officer commanding Engineering Wing was initially Wing Commander (later Air Commodore) Peter Giles and then Wing Commander Chris Elkins, and for my final few weeks in command, by Wing Commander Martin Marlow-Spalding. Administrative Wing was initially headed by Wing Commander (later Group Captain) Tim Pink and he was succeeded by Wing Commander Rob Littlejohn. Of special note, No. 15 Squadron of the RAF Regiment was led by Squadron Leader Graham Stacey (later Air Marshal Sir Graham). The RAF Regiment was an impressive squadron. I had a great team.

Being station commander was my most enjoyable tour of duty. The job was multi-varied and full of activity. It was nice to be the one in charge of the train set and to make the decisions, it very much suited my style and gave me a lot of personal satisfaction. I obviously had all the responsibility on base but I also had many representational responsibilities off base as well, and the station hosted many important visits, from politicians to dignitaries from overseas, by the chief of the Air Staff and many other senior officers from all three services, and many others. A frequent visitor was Prince Bernhard of the Netherlands. He used to come to partake in sporting activities in north Yorkshire. He almost felt like a personal friend and, to my surprise, he even called me for a chat one weekend at my residence.

Princess Margaret was the honorary royal air commodore for Leeming. She visited the station during my tour and was excellent and interested company. I do, however, remember one incident that followed her visit. She had very kindly planted a tree outside the officers' mess. The morning after her visit, as I arrived at my office to start another day, two of the bachelors who lived in the officers' mess were, sheepishly, standing outside my door waiting to speak with me. The conversation went something like this: "Good morning, Sir." I returned the greeting. They continued, "Sir, we have a confession to make... you remember the tree that our royal visitor planted?" "Yes," I replied. "Well Sir, we burnt it down last night after a bit of a party."

I have to admit, privately, I could see the funny side and I had plenty of my own experience of doing things that I should not have done. However, they knew that they had to be punished and they spent the next month sharing the station role of 'duty officer'. I very much liked the two officers concerned, they had spirit and they were also good at their respective jobs. The tree was replaced and most people, in all probability, would not have known what had happened. All a part of life!

I also used to like my quarterly 'get togethers' in the sergeants' mess with all of the warrant officers on the station. There were usually in excess of 20 at these 'Chatham House Rule' meetings. I found the meetings to be of exceptional value and they gave me an excellent insight into the state of my station, where there were problems etc. In short, it helped me to keep my finger on the pulse. There was also a valuable social side to the occasions and I know they appreciated the access that the meetings gave to me as station commander.

I must also mention the community side to my time as station commander. First, there were an excellent, and very lively, group of honorary members of the officers' mess, some of whom were local farmers. I must make special mention of two, John Penty and John Fall. John Penty and his wife, Jenny, and their family, all became close personal friends and we remain in contact to this day. John Fall, I remember, in particular, for the occasional bridge party that he would hold at his magnificent house, not because of the bridge per se but because of the size of the whiskies that he would pour to fuzz our brains. Yorkshire is a wonderful county with beautiful scenery. Leeming sits in between the Yorkshire Dales and the Moors, there was no shortage of things to do and places to see and the pubs were all very special. We became friendly with so many wonderful people including the sheriff of North Yorkshire, the leader of the North Yorkshire District Council and also the chief constable, all good people. I must also make special mention of the mayor of Bedale at the time, a well-known vet called Lewis Grant. Lewis was a man of great humour and amongst much socialising we also used to play golf at Bedale where I witnessed Lewis achieve a hole in one – with a difference. He 'duffed' his shot off the tee and the ball rolled along the ground all the way to the green, then continued to roll on to the green and into the hole. I have never seen a hole in one from a worse shot. We celebrated and laughed about the story for weeks.

After a wonderful tour, I handed over command of Leeming in late June 1992 to another old friend and colleague, Group Captain Phil Roser. Phil and I had first met back in my Lightning days at RAF Coltishall where I was his instructor before he went on to my old squadron, No. 92 Squadron, at Gütersloh. I had a memorable what I thought would be my last ever flight in a Tornado. It was a one versus one air combat sortie with an old colleague from Coningsby days, now the weapons instructor on No. 25 Squadron, Squadron Leader (later Air Commodore) Mark Swan. It was a good fight and I could think of no better way to end my flying career. Little was I to know, at that time, that less than two years later I would again be flying the Tornado. Mark himself went on to have a very successful later career as a director and board member of the Civil Aviation Authority. My last day in charge of Leeming was also memorable for another reason. Ian Botham, the well-known cricketer and charity walker for leukaemia, had at last managed to find the time in his busy programme to visit Leeming. He had a great day and I was able to be with him off and on during his visit when I was not involved in handover tasks. Ian also flew in a Tornado. I handed over command at about four thirty p.m., as I recall, and Phil was happy for me to go to the bar to have a beer with Ian even though I was no longer the station commander. We did just that, in fact we had several beers and Ian also witnessed No. 11 Squadron having a bit of a celebration, I forget what about, which ended in a traditional burning of an old piano which was no longer of any use. There has long been a tradition in the RAF for the burning of old pianos on certain squadrons.

Finally, one other story from my time at Leeming. As station commander I would regularly entertain in my residence and on one occasion The Right Honourable William Hague, at the time our local Member of Parliament, was coming to dinner. Well, he duly arrived but to Tina and my surprise, 20 minutes early. Tina had more on than I, I recall, and had quickly to put on enough clothes to look decent and rush downstairs to welcome William, whom we already knew from other social occasions. We have chuckled about that evening on many occasions but I don't think that William ever realised that he was so early.

Another chapter in my life came to a close, a memorable one, and now it was off to the next adventure, this time to prepare to move to America to take up my next appointments. However, for my leadership at Leeming and in the Gulf, I was honoured to be appointed a Commander of the British Empire (CBE) in the 1993 Queen's New Year Honours List.

CHAPTER 12
AMERICAN ADVENTURE

I did not expect to be asked to go to America as the assistant air attaché and deputy commander of RAF Staff at the British embassy in Washington because I had not previously served in America on an exchange posting. However, I was delighted to be given the opportunity. I took up my new position in November 1992, the same month that Bill Clinton was elected to be president.

After my departure from Leeming I spent the period from June to November 1992 attending courses and being briefed by a number of RAF organisations and government departments in preparation for my new appointment. There was also a large amount of domestic organisation to be done, a house to let, children to sort at school, belongings to send in advance to America or to put in storage, new uniforms to buy, even glasses and china to procure for the large amount of entertaining that we were expected to do. For example, we were advised to make sure that we had sufficient good china and crystal glasses for a sit-down dinner of up to 16 people. It was a busy few months but it was also pleasant to have those few months living back in our house in the lovely village of Wistow, near Huntingdon in Cambridgeshire, and without all the responsibility that I had had at Leeming. In short, it was a welcome opportunity to re-charge the batteries and to relax. Our neighbours in Wistow were a great bunch, we were all about the same age and we liked a good party. Rod and Adrienne, Brian and Cathryn, Ed and Patricia, Terry and Eleanor, Angus and Julia to name but a few of my fellow villagers. On Friday nights we boys would go to the village pub from which we would usually return at a time way after the official pub closing time and usually via one of our houses for a nightcap or two. I did so much enjoy living in that village but I am not sure about my three children who were growing up fast and would have preferred, I am sure, to be living somewhere where there was more social opportunity for their age groups.

In November 1992, we flew to Washington and spent the first two weeks living in a hotel before moving into our ex-officio residence in Maclean, Virginia, a lovely house and an ideal place for entertaining.

I had known many of my Washington staff for a number of years, they were a talented group who covered most of the various specialisations, The defence attaché was Air Vice-Marshal Peter Dodworth, a Harrier pilot who I had first met when he was an instructor at RAF Valley when I did my advanced flying training. We remain good friends to this day. The air attaché was Air Commodore Simon Baldwin, a great character with an excellent brain and more than a zest for life. I really enjoyed my time working alongside Simon and also sharing considerable time in each other's social company and on the golf course. Simon's wife, Sheila was also great company and fun. They certainly knew how to party.

On arrival at the British embassy I had an audience with the then ambassador, Sir Robin Renwick, and met all the diplomatic staff. I well remember when I had my initial meeting with Sir Robin, there was a big map of America behind his desk. Superimposed over the state of Texas was a scale map of Great Britain. This put into immediate perspective the difference in the size of the two countries and made a lasting impact.

My time in America was packed full of variety. There has always been a close relationship between the British Armed Forces and the American services and I spent a fair amount of time in the Pentagon liaising primarily with the United States Air Force staff but also with elements from the other services. From a London perspective we were very much regarded as an extension of the Ministry of Defence and sometimes referred to as MoD West. I also travelled a lot because I had a responsibility for all the RAF on exchange or secondment in the United States and this amounted to a significant number spread far and wide in the United States. America is a big place and I travelled the length and breadth of the country, from Florida to Alaska, from Texas to New York. This gave me the opportunity to get to know the big country properly. There is a great difference between the various states, from topography to culture and it is a fascinating place. When I visited exchange officers at their bases, I also had the opportunity to see the activities associated with the unit task, to meet the people, to socialise and often to fly. It was a wonderful experience. I flew a number of times in the F-16 and in a number of helicopters, and also a memorable low-level sortie in a giant C-5 Galaxy.

I recall one particular flight from the US Naval Base at Whidbey Island. I flew a sortie in a Grumman A-6 Intruder aircraft, which I remember because a fire warning light came on and I was asked to tighten my straps for a possible ejection. Well, I didn't have to eject and the navy pilot with whom I was flying landed the aircraft without further incident at a remote airfield called Yakima from where I was collected by another aircraft some hours later and flown back to Whidbey Island. However, there had been a few tense moments during the emergency.

The air attaché world was an interesting experience and an opportunity to meet many other attachés from all over the globe. Almost every night there were functions to attend, sometimes as many as three or four. Life was busy and I remember how one enjoyed the occasional evening off when there was an opportunity to relax. I also wore an array of uniforms, air force blue in the winter, khaki in the summer plus a white ceremonial uniform with plenty of gold in evidence for formal receptions.

I met a lot of well-known people during my time in Washington, senior air force officers from many countries, leaders in business and big names in the global context. In particular, I remember Nelson Mandela visiting the capital and attending a reception in the British embassy. I could immediately see for myself his statesmanlike qualities. A tall man, he had great presence.

Our three children were all at boarding school in the UK and we certainly missed most being able to see them more often. They used to fly out for the school holidays and we had some wonderful holidays whilst in America, there was so much to see and I know they absolutely loved these adventures. They saw Disneyland and many other holiday experiences in Florida all the way down to Key West, we had a fantastic three-week holiday on the West Coast plus visits to the Grand Canyon, and trips to New York to name but a few. We often used to use the holiday facilities available at air force and navy locations, excellent places which were available to us at minimal cost.

Work-wise, as well as all the travel within America I also returned to the UK on occasions for liaison and briefing purposes and I also used to go to New York once a month to attend meetings at the United Nations where I was a member of the United Nations Military Staff Committee. When I departed America, I was presented with a plaque thanking me for my contribution to the committee. The truth was that it was useless and sterile. The members were representatives from the countries which sat on the United Nations Security Council. The committee never made any decisions for the simple reason that the United States or Russia would always veto the decision of each other. It was an eye-opening experience and I would like to think that that is no longer the case.

Our time in Washington was cut short when I was informed that I was to be promoted to air commodore and would be returning to the UK to become the RAF's Inspector of Flight Safety. I was naturally delighted to be told about the promotion, and of course it was also going to bring us closer to the children, but at the same time I was going to be sad to leave America after only 16 months in post. There were financial advantages to remaining in America and there were things that I wanted still to do both at work and in the country at large. For example, America is a very large country with 52 states. Thus far I had seen 32 of these states, not a bad total in the short time that I had been there, but I was sorry not to see those parts that I had not yet visited. The children were also sorry that there would be no more special holidays.

The climate in Washington was also interesting. The winters can oscillate between very cold and quite warm and the summers are invariably hot and humid. For me, this was never demonstrated better than when in March 1994 I had my farewell party on the deck of the residence. On the previous day there had been a big snowstorm and the snow was still very evident. However, the temperature was now over 60 degrees and we were all enjoying the sunshine on my deck in shirt sleeves with the thawing snow still around us, something that I will never forget. Other memories about the weather were the ice-storms that we experienced and the differences in the seasons between Washington and London. In Washington, there is a winter and summer but the spring and autumn seemed to happen very quickly and spring, in particular, always occurred in April and lasted little more than a week.

There were other events which I remember. I recall the occasion when the air attaché was overseas for a couple of weeks. When this happened, I would have the use of his Lincoln car. On this occasion, there had been a heavy snowstorm in Washington. When this happened, we were unable to drive our cars up the hill to the main road. Our house sat at the bottom of a steep cul-de-sac. On such occasions, we would park a car in our neighbour's drive from which we had access to the road. I entered the drive to pre-position the Lincoln but the drive was so icy that the car could not be stopped and slid into a ditch. I felt such an idiot and was highly embarrassed. The car was then off the road for a few weeks whilst the damage was repaired. Fortunately, Simon Baldwin, the air attaché, was a very understanding man. However, my pride was dented.

On another occasion, I was flying to Los Angeles to visit several RAF exchange officers based on, or close to, the West Coast, a flight of at least four hours from Washington. The flight was first delayed in Washington because Los Angeles had experienced a major earthquake, but did eventually depart about four hours later. It was not the flight itself that was eventful, however. I remember arriving at Los Angeles airport and, whilst waiting for a small commuter aircraft to fly to another town in California, I experienced an aftershock of the earthquake. This itself was far greater than I expected and to me it felt like what I always thought an earthquake would be like. Los Angeles is situated on a fault line and this was not the first time that there had been an earthquake there but it was the first time that I had been involved. I do not wish to repeat the experience. The damage to infrastructure around Los Angeles was very severe.

Washington is an interesting city and, like most other big cities in the world, there are no-go areas. Now, it was easy to take a wrong turning such is the design of access roads. These can be very confusing. We found ourselves in undesirable parts of town on more than one occasion. You can feel very vulnerable until you find your way out of the area. On one occasion, at a traffic light, the driver of an adjacent car even warned us that we were in a dangerous area and to get out as quickly as possible. We did!

We enjoyed being in Washington, an interesting and lovely city, and we enjoyed all that we did and saw in America. The experience gave me a good insight into the diplomatic world which I found both interesting and educational. It was fascinating to see diplomacy at work. I was also interested to find that, invariably, we were dealing with information and issues, sometimes several days before they would appear in the media, and sometimes this never happened. I found myself to be well-informed and overall it was a very rewarding experience.

So, in March 1994, we returned to the UK to be followed by our goods and chattels, and a new tax-free Volvo, to begin the next exciting stage in my career.

CHAPTER 13
INSPECTOR OF RAF FLIGHT SAFETY

I would like to open this chapter on my time as Inspector of Flight Safety with a tribute to the very first Inspector of RAF Flight Safety, a man who I knew well and who had been my commander in No. 11 (Fighter) Group, and a man for whom I had the greatest respect. His name was Air Marshal Sir Kenneth Hayr.

Air Marshal Sir Kenneth Hayr lost his life, aged 66, in a flying display accident at Biggin Hill on 2nd June 2001. He was a valued friend to me and respected as one of the best pilots in the service. He held senior positions in the RAF during the Falklands campaign – in which his planning role was significant – and the Gulf War. We shared an abiding passion: piloting aircraft and, in particular, fighter aircraft.

Born in St. Helier, New Zealand in 1935, he attended RAF College, Cranwell. He honed his fighter skills on the Hawker Hunter and English Electric Lightning, both close to my heart. Subsequently, he was appointed Phantom OCU squadron commander, Coningsby, and latterly he took command of No. 1 (Fighter) Squadron in Cambridgeshire. He later recalled his experiences on the VTOL Harrier in the history of the squadron... "Every dog has its day and this was the time of my life because it was the most exhilarating, interesting and fantastic period in the peacetime life of a squadron commander." How right he was...

I eventually followed him as the RAF's Inspector of Flight Safety between 1994 and 1997. He had been IFS from 1976 to 1979. It could not have suited him better, providing opportunities to fly as frequently as his duties permitted.

Chairman of the New Zealand Aviation Trust, he was also appointed AFC in 1963 and Bar in 1972; CBE in 1976; CB in 1982; KCB in 1988; KBE in 1991. He was awarded the Kuwait Liberation Order 1st Grade in the same year.

At Biggin Hill, flying a de Havilland Vampire, he was displaying the aircraft when he had his accident with, unfortunately, fatal results.

Ken was a courteous and popular man who remained in spirit a fighter pilot to the last...

In my role as Inspector of Flight Safety, I reported to the assistant chief of the Air Staff (ACAS) but I also had a direct line to the chief of the Air Staff (CAS). I was responsible for all RAF flight safety policy and post-crash management. My organisation, which numbered about 35 personnel, was initially based in London at MoD Adastral House but during my tour I rusticated it out to RAF Bentley Priory in north-west London. All those on my staff had a key responsibility in their specialist areas but I must single out two roles as being of greatest importance, those of the deputy Inspector of Flight Safety, who was effectively my chief of Staff, and the Engineering Inspector of Flight Safety, a job always filled by a top-quality engineering officer.

As an air commodore this was a dream job: I travelled widely, I flew most RAF aircraft and I kept closely in touch with the people. It was a fascinating job and I certainly had my eyes opened wide when I saw the demands of the various operational roles. In particular, I found helicopter flying in Northern Ireland very interesting, as I did flying with the Hercules Special Forces low level at night in Wales, and the Nimrod, also at night and very low level over the sea. I completed a helicopter course at RAF Shawbury and then flew all helicopters in service. I remained current first pilot on the Tornado F3, Hawk, Tucano and C-130 Hercules.

Flight safety emerged in response to a general alarm about aircraft crashes. The interruption of WWI in the natural development of aviation, so soon after the first flight, diverted attention from aircraft accidents and it was not until 1920 that the government appointed an Inspector of Accidents as part of the directorate of Civil Aviation. In 1937, an Accidents Investigation Board was formed under the auspices of a director general of aviation. In 1942 the RAF took on the responsibility for investigating their own accidents.

Since WWII the overall RAF accident rate has very significantly improved. In 1946 the RAF lost 337 aircraft in the UK and over 1,000 aircraft all over the world, statistics that are not only eye opening but we also tend to forget. By the 1970s the number of aircraft lost was around 40 per year and by the 1990s this figure had further reduced to single figure numbers, and they continue to reduce to the present day. There are many contributors to this improvement but to me the most important factor is the role and influence of flight safety.

I was delighted, indeed elated, to be the RAF Inspector of Flight Safety, it was a job where I certainly felt like 'a round peg in a round hole'. My job revolved around two of my big likes, namely flying and people. It was a very stimulating experience. I had a great staff and we achieved much, from moving the inspectorate from London, overseeing important changes to Board of

Inquiry procedures, introducing a more honest and open reporting environment, the carrying out of specific aircraft safety reviews and many other important initiatives which 'made a difference'. The downside of the job were the accidents, all of which were investigated and all too often the findings related to human factor causes or, put another way, many accidents could have been avoided.

There was a lot of change taking place in London in the 1990s with regard to the number of buildings being used for MoD purposes. The building in which we were located, Adastral House, was to be closed and at least two investment appraisals were carried out to identify a suitable location for the Inspectorate of Flight Safety. Finally, a decision was made to move the organisation to RAF Bentley Priory, a delightful place not too far from the RAF Museum. Importantly, as far as I was concerned, it was historically the home of Fighter Command, my alma mater, and I was naturally delighted with this decision. I appointed a project officer, John Chapman, who did an outstanding job of managing the move. I remember enquiring about the budget that we had for the move and how it was to be broken down. I was informed that there was simply a lump sum allocated for us to manage and this was music to my ears because it meant that we could make the decisions without having to seek the approval of other departments. As a result, we were able to make best use of the funds for our purposes.

At Bentley Priory, we moved into our own building which had been prepared for the move including the preparation of a purpose-built lecture theatre from where many of the courses run by the inspectorate, those such as the flight safety course, flying authorisers course, flying control committee course, to name but some, could be managed. This theatre was named the 'Hayr Theatre' and I was delighted that Ken Hayr himself, the first IFS, was able to carry out the initial opening. It was also an appropriate occasion to have a reunion of as many previous holders as possible of the Inspector of Flight Safety appointment, and there was one other important event that took place on the same day that is worthy of mention. Martin-Baker is a company with which anyone involved with military aviation can closely identify. I for one spent my whole flying career sitting on a Martin-Baker ejection seat and it was always a fact that gave me great comfort, the knowledge that I had the capability to eject from my aircraft as a last resort. Over 7,000 aircrew owe their lives to this excellent company, still to this day privately owned. A member of the bigger Martin-Baker family, Sarah Sharman, a lawyer and Cambridge graduate with a strong interest in aviation and, in particular, the history and achievements of the Martin-Baker Company, had written a book on the life of the founder of the company, the legendary Sir James Martin. The occasion was used to publicise the book and to honour the achievements of the company. Sarah herself had hoped to fly and had joined the Cambridge University Air Squadron but her hopes were somewhat dashed when she was involved in a car accident whilst at Cambridge which seriously damaged her back, and her hopes to fly. I was personally delighted that we were able to honour the achievements of a great company on this occasion.

Boards of Inquiry were an important part of the flight safety scene, and every accident was investigated by a Board of Inquiry convened by the controlling authority for the aircraft involved. Here was the first disagreement that I had with the system because it effectively meant that the controlling authority was to some extent both the judge and jury. I always considered that there should be an independent organisation that conducted these inquiries but that part of the system did not change during my watch. However, I am very pleased to see that the change has since been made.

I was also very concerned about the overall Board of Inquiry procedures and, in particular, relating to the consideration and allocation of blame. I was aware that the flying community at large considered there to be a blame culture in evidence and they had a case. I could see that Boards of Inquiry, in general, seemed to be spending an inordinate amount of time involved with the consideration and allocation of blame when the primary purpose of the inquiry should be to determine the cause of the accidents. To me the system was wrong and so I put forward a paper to the assistant chief of Air Staff which proposed that a review be carried out of Board of Inquiry procedures. It just so happened that, at the same time, I also became aware that the army had similar concerns about Boards of Inquiry. A review was ordered and took place, a report was submitted and the recommendations were accepted. The most notable of these recommendations was the proposal to remove the allocation of blame from the Board of Inquiry procedure, and a suggestion that if there was considered a legal case to answer then this should become the subject of a separate legal inquiry. This was accepted and, in my view, this has since had a profound effect. Any concern about a blame culture was removed and the emphasis of future inquiries would now, rightly, concentrate on accident investigation. Human factors rightly formed a part of the investigation but no allocation of blame.

The above changes, unfortunately, were not retrospective which meant that any allocation of blame from earlier accident investigations remained extant.

Probably the most significant of these was the Mull of Kintyre Chinook accident in 1994 which was given so much publicity and attention for many years before the allocation of blame decisions made in that inquiry were finally overturned. Had the new procedures been introduced before this accident then a lot of angst on all sides could have been avoided.

I was determined to see eliminated any form of blame culture. The changes to Boards of Inquiry procedure were obviously an important development but there was also the reporting of incidents to consider. I was aware that there were also many who considered that here too there was too much attention given to the allocation of blame. The effect of this was that incidents, in some cases, were not being properly reported and air events that took place and from which everyone could learn were being kept quiet, a situation which was not helpful to anyone and at the most extreme could be hiding dangerous influences on accidents. And so, we introduced an honest and open reporting system which did not carry any allocation of blame. This too, in my view, was a great success, much was learnt, everyone seemed to be happier with the system and people talked openly instead of concealing information.

I have always been a thinker about the way ahead for everything in life and this was no less the case for the management of flight safety. Whilst Inspector of Flight Safety I used to liaise closely with organisations such as the Civil Aviation Authority (CAA), the Aircraft Accident Investigation Board (AAIB) and British Airways. These associations focused my mind. For example, I asked myself why we didn't have a military aviation authority to match the CAA. The individual services looked after their own flight safety and that was fine but I felt that there was the requirement to link more closely. I could see the need for a defence aviation safety organisation as an interim measure prior to forming a military aviation authority. I wrote a paper to say as much but I was not allowed to progress my ideas because of single-service interests. At the time I was disappointed because I knew that it would eventually happen and I am delighted that that has proven to be the case.

IFS had responsibility for the flight safety magazine *Air Clues*, a first-class publication at the time which was an excellent forum for transmitting the safety messages and stories. The infamous, but fictitious, Wing Commander Spry managed the publication and would write his own well-read column. In practice, Wing Commander Spry was actually a squadron leader member of my staff who had been identified with an ability to write. I also used to write a column 'The Inspector Says'. Another well-known article in the magazine was called 'I learnt about flying from that'. These were true stories written by RAF aircrew and were always fascinating to read. In fact, so enthusiastic was I about these stories that we produced a book with the same title with the foreword written by Richard Branson. Making contact with Richard to ask him to write the foreword was a major task in its own right, so difficult was it to get to his inner circle. I have long felt that an annual book under the same title could be produced and would sell well but as yet this has not happened. Maybe someone will now take the hint.

I am not going to write about all the accidents that occurred in my watch, suffice to say that all are catalogued elsewhere in books, journals and reports. However, so many of these accidents were unnecessary and I was surprised by the number that happened in what I would call 'low arousal' situations, i.e. not during the high-pressure situations in which military pilots find themselves all the time. Also, so many were preventable which were primarily caused by human factor failings. In this area I found the contribution and advice of the psychologist who advised IFS, Dr John Chappelow, to be absolutely invaluable and if there is one area where maximum effort always needs to be directed in the cause of accident prevention then it is human error. It is such an interesting area to study.

Among many memorable assignments I must single out for special mention a visit to Australia in 1995, at the invitation of the then Australian chief of Air Staff, Air Marshal Les Fisher, to carry out an audit of flight safety in the Royal Australian Air Force (RAAF). The RAAF had endured a bad period of accidents. I spent a very interesting and stimulating month in Australia and submitted my report with over 200 recommendations. I was delighted when it was accepted in full and the recommendations then gradually implemented. Of great importance, however, is the fact that the accident rate plummeted and has remained at a low level to this day. As an achievement, it has always given me a feeling of great pride. I also commend the chief of the RAAF for inviting me to carry out an audit of his air force from the flight safety perspective, a brave initiative and one that was highly successful.

During my time as IFS I travelled widely including to the US, Canada, Australia, India and South Africa in addition to many European countries. I always found these visits to be useful for the exchange of information and ideas, and to compare the issues of the day. To some people, these trips were considered to be an expensive luxury but I would disagree, they were always invaluable. We can all learn from each other and such visits were often the source of new ideas which helped to prevent accidents and thus save money.

I was chairman of the European Air Forces Flight Safety Committee which used to meet twice a year in a different country for each meeting. There were 27 countries represented on this committee and it was a very useful forum on which to compare the issues and learn about each other. I personally found it to be an important and useful committee and it was a responsibility which I greatly enjoyed. Mind you, I will also never forget one very sad occasion when we were convening in Toronto. Our meeting had been arranged to coincide with the Toronto Air Show on the Saturday. It was at that air show that I witnessed the RAF display Nimrod crash into Lake Ontario with the awful loss of seven lives. This is not the place to go into the detail of the occasion but suffice to say that it was a very low point, and an event which I often re-live in my mind.

An important element of the inspectorate's work were the reviews that were conducted into all aspects of the operation of specific aircraft types. Specialist teams were usually attached to my organisation for the duration of the review, a period that could last for up to six months. Very detailed reports were written and then circulated for comment and action. There were always a very large number of recommendations to be considered. The upside to these reviews was the fact that they took place at all. In my view, they contributed significantly to the safe operation of the aircraft reviewed. The downside was that each survey took time and there were insufficient resources available to carry out more than one aircraft review at a time. It would have been of added benefit if more aircraft could have been inspected on a more regular basis.

An important aspect of my time as Inspector of Flight Safety was the confidential reporting system that I alone ran, and which was called CONDOR. Anyone in the RAF could complete a CONDOR form, readily available at bases, and then send by post direct to me and marked 'Confidential for Addressee'. They could also phone a secure telephone number which was only accessible by me. I used to receive, on average, about 25 such reports per year. The most important thing was always to protect the confidentiality of the individual which usually meant that any research had to be conducted in a very discreet manner. The reports used to cover a range of subjects, most of the time related to aircraft or system problems but also concerning individual interference or other personal or personnel problems. These were the hardest to research. I would always respond direct to the author of the report to convey my views or intentions, or to give advice on further action. CONDOR was a very successful system from which much was learnt about problems.

I found the subject of relationships to be an interesting area. First, I must say that my dealings were always exceptional with my own staff. Whilst I tended to spend a lot of the time on visits to units, speaking to people and flying, my deputy, initially Group Captain Martin 'Dim' Jones and then Group Captain Peter Gooding both did an outstanding job and managed the office in my absence. I can't speak too highly of their contribution and they both remain good friends to this day.

I found that I also developed excellent relationships with the units and RAF at large. I felt in touch with the people, I listened to their issues and concerns and I understood them and did my best to help. Likewise, I learnt a lot from the flying side and again understood the problems and concerns. During my time these particularly revolved around factors such as fatigue. Where I found life a little more difficult was in convincing those above me of the various problems that I was hearing about and where I also found that some very senior officers were less than sympathetic. I think they also felt that I was getting too close to the air force beneath me, this is true but they needed someone to listen and I did. I certainly found myself identifying with their problems but it is funny how sometimes an office in London can make one lose sight of what is going on in the wider world outside.

I have said it already but I loved this job and I have had a close interest and involvement with aviation safety ever since my nearly four years as IFS. This period was a time of great satisfaction but also some frustration in my attempts to get things changed or heard. RAF flight safety has come a long way since World War II, and although in the financial reckoning cost savings are to a degree unquantifiable, they are substantive. I look back at my time as Inspector of Flight Safety with mainly satisfaction and pleasure, and I am happy in my own mind that we achieved much and saved lives.

CHAPTER 14
A SHORT TIME WITH EUROFIGHTER AND FAREWELL RAF

As I left my post as Inspector of Flight Safety, I was conscious of the fact that I was now on my last lap in the RAF and I was very much beginning to think of my future. My wife had started a physiotherapy degree course at Southampton University and I had put in a request that I remain in the London area for my final job, ideally at the MoD, for family reasons. I was quite surprised, therefore, when I received a phone call to say that the chief of the Air Staff (CAS) wanted me to go to Scotland to become the Air Officer Scotland and Northern Ireland (AOSNI) which was double-hatted with an air commodore appointment as station commander RAF Leuchars, a fighter station that I knew well and loved.

Normally, I would have jumped at such an opportunity but I declined the offer for a number of reasons: I did not wish to disturb my wife's university course and I did not think that I could do the job justice without her accompanying me to Scotland. I had already completed a very successful station commander tour at RAF Leeming and, finally, at the time, and from a personal perspective, I did not actually agree with the decision to combine the two jobs. CAS twice asked me to take the job but, for better or worse, my mind was made up and I stuck to my decision. To this day, I often muse on this decision because there was so much to gain from taking the job – a command appointment, more flying the Tornado F3, and also flying the Bulldog with the resident air experience flight, playing golf at St Andrews, being in Scotland, the great social life and, yes, I do have my regrets but that is life.

I was then selected for a new job in the MoD on which I had had my eyes for some time, to become director of the Eurofighter Typhoon introduction to service programme. Having introduced the Tornado F2/3 into RAF service I was in an ideal position and I was initially delighted at the appointment for what would be my last couple of years in the RAF. As it turned out, the job did not give me the overall satisfaction that I had expected, mainly because I did not have adequate resources available. I had a very good staff officer to assist, Wing Commander Nick Watson (later Air Commodore) and an outstanding warrant officer, Mark Edy (who was later commissioned), to support me with the task but it was an uphill struggle to get it properly established, and to get financial approval for additional resources. Also, I did not have the control over the overall programme that I would have liked. However, it was an experience and I am not complaining, and by that time I was also being contacted by industry concerning my future employment.

My job as director of the Eurofighter Typhoon introduction to service was an important one. As the chief of the Air Staff reminded me as I took up the position, and in his own words: "Eurofighter Typhoon is the largest and most expensive modern programme in which the RAF has ever been involved and it is essential that we get the introduction into service right." Four nations – the UK, Germany, Italy and Spain – were involved in the programme. As with the multi-national Tornado programme there were both upsides and downsides to this type of programme. On the upside, it was good for interoperability, and cost and work sharing, and it forged new and good relationships within both the military and industry. On the downside, it sometimes meant that decisions could be slow in being made, which was because the agreement of all four nations would have to be sought and given and there were, on occasions, political obstacles to decisions. However, also on the plus side, it did mean infrequent trips to Munich, Rome or Madrid. At that time, the UK was to buy 232 Typhoons, mainly to replace the Jaguar and Tornado F3. This number has since been reduced as a result of various defence reviews. One aspect that I found very interesting was that, out of the 232 aircraft to be bought, around 89 were included in the figure as attrition aircraft, a procurement number to take into account a projected number of aircraft that could be expected to be lost over a 25-year timescale. As has since been proven, this number was far too many and, if one looks at the cost, it could be argued, an unaffordable luxury.

I never flew the Typhoon. At the time that I was in post, there were a total of seven prototype aircraft involved with the development programme which was then in progress between the four nations. The programme was already running late and if I had a flight it could have given industry the perfect excuse for further delay. I would obviously have liked to fly the aircraft but I did at least fly the simulator.

Plans for the introduction to service were frequently subject to change, either because of delays, changes in plans or a variety of other reasons. It was a very big programme and there was a lot to take into consideration. In the UK, the delivery of the aircraft was but one aspect of the programme. As I recall, there were a total of 11 separate organisations involved in the introduction to service, all with an important part to play. The programme was a considerable co-ordination exercise and I used to spend a fair amount of time on the road between organisations.

There were two aspects of the Eurofighter Typhoon programme that I would also like briefly to mention. The first is the subject of squadron number plates. This subject can and does get very tribal. In an age when there are not many flying squadrons left in the RAF there are some very proud and famous squadron numbers that people do their very best to protect. This is totally understandable but I was surprised to see, in the short time in which I was involved with the programme, the squadron number plate details for the coming Typhoon force change more than once or twice. There was also an interesting and prolonged discussion about the name for Eurofighter before the name Typhoon was chosen. This was due, mainly, because there was sensitivity about the name. It is also an example of how the need to achieve four-nation agreement can delay decisions.

I left the RAF at age 54 but I had had many opportunities to leave over the years, at age option points during my career, and also to apply for redundancy programmes as the RAF rapidly reduced in size. In general, I loved my life in the RAF and that was the main reason why I stayed. I had also had some fantastic jobs and postings which meant that I would have been daft to leave. When I was Inspector of Flight Safety there had been a very attractive redundancy programme which made me almost decide to apply to leave. In fact, I had written my letter of application which I never submitted for a number of reasons. I was enjoying too much my time as Inspector of Flight Safety and I had an excellent team who I did not want to let down by deserting the sinking ship. I also had three children at a very expensive boarding school for which I was receiving financial assistance from the RAF, and so I stayed. Had I been able to stay in the RAF until I was 60 or even 65, still with the opportunity to be promoted, I think I would have probably remained, but that option was not available to me in full-time service at the time.

When I joined the RAF in 1965, from South Africa, I was too old to go to Cranwell and I enlisted on an eight-year short-service commission. Not knowing what lay ahead, I did not want to commit myself to any longer period. The rest is history. I was switched to a general list commission halfway through my first operational tour and, now, after almost 35 years of service it was time to leave. I had had a quite magnificent career in the RAF, I could never have foreseen what lay ahead when I joined, who can, but I would do it all over again if I could. In joining the RAF, I entered an organisation that gave me a career that I loved and I was probably fortunate that, after a tentative start pre-solo on my basic flying course, I took to flying like a duck to water. I became a fighter pilot like my father and I flew some magnificent high-performance aircraft, I rose to the rank of air commodore and I had some wonderful jobs. There were a number of firsts in my career and these have mainly been covered in earlier chapters. I was the first pilot to fly both the Tornado F2 and F3 in service. I was the first Tornado fast-jet pilot to fly the Tornado F2 in the now well-known Tornado/Spitfire synchronised air display. I was the first commander to deploy to the Middle East, after Saddam Hussein had invaded Kuwait in 1990, during the build-up to the First Gulf war. Finally, I was the first incumbent in the newly established director of Eurofighter Typhoon introduction to service position in the MoD.

There is no better feeling than to experience the freedom that one gets flying your own aircraft, the pure joy of flying, the three-dimensional freedom of the airspace, the view from your cockpit office and so much more. Flying is like a drug, one becomes addicted, I certainly was and I was always happiest when in the air. I made exactly the right decision to become a pilot, I worked hard and I reaped the rewards.

The people who I met, and with whom I worked were, most but admittedly not all, special, talented, and good. The camaraderie that I enjoyed throughout my career was equally special and I just feel sorry for that large element of society who have never had the opportunity to experience what I can only say was a privilege.

The places that I have been to, all over the world, the squadron detachments, the inter-air force competitions, the opportunities, the challenges – all led to a life of variety and excitement. It was all a thrill from beginning to end and I still enthuse about all that I have had the opportunity to do.

Finally, the sport that I enjoyed, yet another excellent opportunity that the RAF offered. I played a lot of it throughout my career and representational sport in rugby, cricket, hockey, squash, tennis, golf and swimming. In my latter years I also became president of both RAF Squash and RAF Triathlon, responsibilities that both gave me great pleasure. I will always savour my interest and involvement in RAF sport but I know that I will also have a permanent reminder with the osteo-arthritis that I now suffer in my knees and ankles, a legacy mainly of a lot of hard and very competitive squash – lovely memories!

As I left the RAF, I knew that I would always stay connected with my past and that I had had a 35-year experience which had brought me almost total joy. I am sure that I am not alone in saying that the future looked different from the inside security of the RAF than it did from outside the service. I was aware that life was going to be rather different, that I was stepping into the unknown but I was also excited because I knew that new challenges lay ahead. I knew not what these challenges would be, nor how much further excitement and satisfaction was to come in the future. Onwards and upwards, 'Per Ardua Ad Astra'.

CHAPTER 15
LIFE OUTSIDE THE RAF

As I came to my final days in the RAF my attention turned to the next chapter in my life, the outside world. I first had to decide in which direction I wished my career to go, did I want to stay involved with aviation or did I want to explore other avenues? For me the decision was easy. I had had over 30 wonderful years involved with aviation and a career that had brought me total satisfaction. I decided that aviation was where I wanted to stay involved. I had also been in discussions with a number of aerospace companies about employment or rather they had been speaking to me. I nearly went to work for BAE Systems, a company that I had been closely associated with for many years but it just so happened that as I was leaving the RAF they were going through a merger with GEC and there was therefore a lot of turmoil and some significant re-structuring taking place. I could not wait until things settled down, I needed to move straight into a paid job with three children still in education. Separately, I had been approached by a company called Computing Devices which was owned by the giant American aerospace company, General Dynamics. Computing Devices was later re-named General Dynamics UK. I was offered the job of military advisor to take over from another ex-RAF air commodore, Dennis Caldwell, a good friend who was also an ex-Lightning pilot. I accepted the offer. I liked the people that I had met in the company, in particular the UK chairman, Sir Donald Spiers, and the managing director, Jim Juntilla. I had first got to know Sir Donald when, together, we gave a presentation on the Tornado F2/3 to King Hussein, accompanied by King Constantine, at the Farnborough Air Show in the mid-1980s. Sir Donald and I have worked together on a number of occasions since leaving the RAF, he is a good friend and very capable man.

I actually started work with my new company whilst on my terminal RAF leave although I could not be paid until I had officially left the RAF. In fact, I spent an initial three weeks with the company and I don't mind admitting that I found things quite strange, mainly because everything happened in a totally different way from what I had been used to in the RAF. I then went on a business studies course at Manchester Business School which was a part of my resettlement training from the RAF. This was an excellent course and I learnt a lot but, most importantly, it helped me understand all about the different structures to be found in the business world and how they worked. I returned to my new job much the wiser and ready to face the new challenges in my life. To this day I retain an association with Manchester Business School as a member of their alumni and I have gained much from this association.

I spent three-and-a-half years with General Dynamics (GD) UK. At the beginning of 2000 my family and I moved from our married quarter home in Maidenhead, where we had lived for six years, to Sussex where, having sold our house in Huntingdon, we bought a lovely six-bedroom country house called 'Little Lankhurst', on the outskirts of the village of Westfield near Hastings. By this stage, only one of our children, Ian, was still at school, at Bradfield College in Berkshire. Our eldest daughter, Lisa, had graduated from Edinburgh University and had also just got married, in December 1999, before we left Maidenhead. She was now working and living in London. Our second daughter, Jenny, had opted not to take up the university place that she had been offered after leaving Bradfield College and before getting her first major job, had completed a business studies course in London. She moved with us to Sussex where she worked in Hastings. My wife, Tina, had herself graduated from Southampton University in 1999 with an honours degree in Physiotherapy. She had already taken up a physiotherapist appointment at the Conquest Hospital in Hastings. Prior to our move to Sussex, Tina and I had already been commuting, for a couple of months, between Maidenhead and Sussex where we lived in temporary accommodation. Our lives were certainly in a fluid situation.

My company was, at the time that I joined it, located in St Leonards-on-Sea which adjoined Hastings. Work was interesting but different and I don't mind admitting that I missed not having a direct relationship with aeroplanes. The contracts with which I was involved were all to do with avionics. Nevertheless, it was interesting work. I travelled a lot, as far afield as Saudi Arabia and regularly to Switzerland where my old friend and colleague, Kevin Smith, was in charge of the new Pilatus PC-21 aircraft programme. I loved my trips to Switzerland, a very beautiful country, and there was usually a very pleasant social side to these visits. I also kept in close contact with the MoD and I used to meet regularly with military advisors from other companies. In fact, it was these meetings which led me into another initiative which had a very positive outcome. I thought to myself, 'Wouldn't it be a good idea if, instead

of regular one-on-one lunches with the other military advisors we form ourselves into a group and meet collectively a few times per year?' So I arranged
a lunch in a well-known London restaurant near the MoD called Champagne
Charlies and met up with three good friends, Rich Rhodes, Paul Crotty and
Peter Crawford, all of whom were also ex-RAF.

From that meeting, in the year 2000, the Aviation Focus Group, now affectionately known as the AFG, was formed. We initially decided that there
should be three lunches per year and that we would limit the numbers of
members to 12, ideally military advisors from the major companies within
the aviation and aerospace industries. Speakers would be invited from the
military, industry and politics. I was, basically, the founder of the organisation
and I ran the AFG from the start in 2000. Well, unknowingly, it quickly
became clear that we had found a niche in the market because there was great
interest in the group and, instead of limiting the number of members to 12, I
let it grow. Very quickly, by 2001, we had 60 to 70 members and at that point
I thought it was time to form a committee because I was finding the workload
to be heavy for one person, Most, but not all, agreed with the idea and a
committee was formed. I became the chairman and we also decided that we
needed a high-profile president. We unanimously decided that Air Chief
Marshal Sir Richard Johns, a former chief of the Air Staff, who was by now
the Governor of Windsor Castle, was our man. Sir Richard was a popular
man with good presence and he was also a man of great charisma. We were
delighted when he accepted our invitation and he became the first honorary
president of the AFG in I think it must have been 2004.

The organisation has thrived and has continued to grow and evolve. We
tried, unsuccessfully, to limit the membership to 100 and then 200 before
deciding to let it develop and evolve at its own pace. By 2019 the membership
stood at nearly 450 from all three services although mainly ex-RAF. Membership has also been opened up to non-military personnel with an involvement
with the military aviation and aerospace world. Speakers are always very
high profile and their talks conducted under 'Chatham House Rule'. The AFG
is a very popular organisation that meets at the RAF Club for lunches and
dinners and is very highly regarded, not only for the quality of the speakers
but also for the excellent networking opportunities that it provides. Lunches
are also conducted in a very relaxed manner. In short, the organisation has
developed its own character. After many years working very much as a team,
in 2017 both Sir Richard and I handed over our respective roles to Air Chief
Marshal Sir Andrew Pulford, also a former chief of Air Staff, and Air Vice-Marshal Sean Bell. Sir Richard then became president emeritus, and I became

the first vice president of the AFG. I must also make mention of the annual committee meeting which used to be held at Sir Richard's lovely Wiltshire house. This was always a most popular occasion, especially so because of the hospitality provided by Sir Richard and his charming wife, Elizabeth. They used to make us so welcome and lunch was always delicious.

Meanwhile, by the year 2003 General Dynamics UK had significantly grown and changed since I joined the company in late 1999, mainly the result of winning a very significant contract, the Bowman contract to provide equipment to the army. My role had evolved first to become director of government affairs and then director of military advisors. The headquarters of the company had moved from Sussex to Wales and it was now much more army than aerospace focused. I had been somewhat frustrated for some time because, apart from my weekend flying with the Air Experience Flight (AEF) at RAF Benson, I had little other direct contact with aeroplanes.

It was time to move on, especially since I was aware that opportunities were about to appear linked to another multi-billion-pound MoD contract, to provide a new military flying training system (MFTS) for the armed forces. I knew that I was well qualified to become involved in this process because of my experiences as a qualified flying instructor where I had been involved with advanced flying training, and further jobs associated with both flying and operational training as commander of the Tornado F3 Operational Conversion Unit, and various other training related jobs that I had had in the MoD. Two of the consortiums that had been formed for the bid approached me, including the eventual winning consortium. However, mainly because of timing, I accepted the job with the consortium known as Vector Flying Training Services. This consortium initially comprised the companies Kellogg Brown and Root (KBR) and EG and G, an American company owned by another giant US company, URS. Bombardier Aerospace later joined the consortium and, also involved, there were two major companies taken on as strategic supplier partners. They were also global companies, namely Northrop Grumman Information Systems and Flight Safety International.

I was recruited, in late 2003, by EG and G as their director of UK operations but specifically for the MFTS bid. The vice president of EG and G who recruited me, Art Mallamo, who became a good friend, was also involved with the bid and shortly after I joined the company, he found himself working for me when I was appointed the managing director of Vector. Although a little surprised, I was delighted to find myself back in a leadership role, a role which I loved. I had over four very happy years with Vector and led a large team which was full of very experienced aviators and specialists in other fields. MFTS was a fascinating programme in which to be involved. I was right back where I enjoyed myself most, at the heart of the flying community. I was working with many old colleagues from my RAF days and it was particularly nice to be associated again with my old friend, Mike Bruce, with whom I had worked closely in the RAF when involved with both the Phantom and Tornado aircraft.

Work on the bid was challenging and it involved a lot of hard work and writing but it was very interesting. Effectively, in the bid we were being asked to design a completely new flying training system for the armed forces and to introduce the complete system by 2013. I travelled extensively, many times to the US where I visited Randolph Air Force Base in San Antonio, Texas, the main base for United States Air Force flying training, and Fort Rucker, where helicopter training is done on what seemed an industrial scale. Fort Rucker was the home of over 600 helicopters and a number of satellite sites were used for helicopter training. These places were impressive to see. Other places visited in the US were Colorado to see where officer training takes place and also to liaise with Northrop Grumman, and there were a number of visits to the headquarters of EG and G, the company for whom I worked, in Austin, Texas. In Canada I visited at least three times the NATO Flying Training School at Moose Jaw in Saskatchewan, and several Canadian aerospace companies.

RAF flying training units visited included Valley, the home of advanced flying training; Linton-on-Ouse, where basic flying training was carried out; Culdrose in Cornwall and Cranwell, where rear-crew training was done; Barkston Heath in Lincolnshire where elementary flying training is completed; Cranwell again to see multi-engine training and other facilities and, finally, Shawbury in Shropshire where the Defence Helicopter Flying Training School is located. There were many visits to the MoD staffs in London and the Defence Equipment and Supply organisation (DE&S) at Abbey Wood near Bristol, and in Europe to Switzerland, Italy and the Czech Republic to liaise with aircraft manufacturers. It really was all a most pleasant experience and I certainly learnt a lot during my time with Vector. That said, it wasn't all plain sailing and there were the occasional inter-company issues to be resolved and not all of the executives in the wider chain were pleasant to deal with but I am not going to labour those points, suffice to say that I had a great time.

Unfortunately, we did not win the bid even though I personally felt, and still do, that we had the best team, and, in my view, we had done more work than the other two teams. Mind you I cannot confirm that fact, it was an impression gained from being aware of where the other teams had visited and through other discussions. It is also possible that we did more work in preparation than necessary. We had assembled an excellent team of experts, over 50 personnel in total, and this same team was fully ready for the implementation phase once the contract had been signed, had we won. However, we also made mistakes, as the later debrief that I requested from the MoD project managers made us aware. We were significantly more expensive than the winning consortium, Ascent. There were also weaknesses in our partnering arrangements.

I spent the first months of 2008 closing down Vector as a company, not a very pleasant task when things could have been very different. As a parting shot, I have also found it interesting to watch the development of the new system from afar. As I write these words, in 2019, the new MFTS system is still not fully up and running and it won't be for several more years. I am also aware that all is not rosy in the military flying training world, certainly not when those hoping for flying training courses are sometimes having to wait for three to four years to commence their training, such is the backlog in the system. I also hear that it is taking seven or eight years for a fast-jet pilot to reach the front line when it took me just three years. I know how I would have felt under such circumstances. I am certain that that would not have been the case if Vector had remained involved but those are only words which will no doubt be disputed.

So, it was now on to other things and, as it has turned out, it has been a lot of things!

CHAPTER 16
MASTER OF THE HONOURABLE COMPANY OF AIR PILOTS

I first came into contact with the then Guild of Air Pilots and Air Navigators (GAPAN) when I was Inspector of Flight Safety for the RAF. In this post I sat on the committee that considered the nominations for an award, the Sir James Martin Award, which was a major flight safety award. In this capacity I was invited by James Martin, co-managing director of Martin-Baker, to attend the very prestigious trophies and awards banquet held each year in the London Guildhall. To say that it is always a special evening is an understatement, it is, quite simply what I call a 'wow' evening. The Guildhall is a magnificent venue that befits the royalty and heads of state who regularly dine there at state and other functions. The annual GAPAN – now known as the Honourable Company of Air Pilots since Her Majesty Queen Elizabeth bestowed the rare title of 'honourable' on the company – banquet is a major event and, in my view, *the* most prestigious aviation awards ceremony, certainly in the UK but possibly in the world. Up to 700 sit down to dine and often in excess of 25 major trophies and awards are presented by the usually very high profile, often royal, guest of honour. The recipients of the awards often receive standing ovations, in particular when associated with some of the amazing rescues that take place involving aviation. It was, therefore, through my involvement with the Sir James Martin Award that I was introduced to the Air Pilots, a City of London livery company which I finally joined in 1997, a decision that has significantly changed my life since becoming a member.

The Honourable Company of Air Pilots is one of around 110 livery companies that represent many of the trades and professions in existence. The

Air Pilots was founded in 1929 and was granted livery status in 1956. Today there are around 2,100 members of which only 600 are allowed by the Court of Alderman to hold the title 'Liveryman', and it is the largest of all the livery companies. It is number 81 in the list of companies and is known as a modern livery company. The oldest livery company dates back to the 13th century. I know that there are a lot of people who do not know or understand what livery companies do but they are an important part of the City of London 'Square Mile' and it is liverymen who every year elect the lord mayor and the two sheriffs of London. I must also add that livery companies are very different from and nothing to do with masonry. They are purely associated with their respective trades and professions but there is also a strong involvement with charity.

After joining the Air Pilots, it quickly opened up new doors and horizons. The membership came from all parts of aviation and it provided me with the opportunity to meet many new faces from the commercial and general aviation sectors as well as from the military which I already knew well. Importantly, the Air Pilots was all about flying, the subject that had been so close to my heart for most of my life. There were also new functions to attend, the opportunity to visit places and organisations associated with aviation that I had not seen. It opened up a new chapter in my life, one that was to become even more important in the future.

Normally, you have to have been a member of the Air Pilots for at least five years before you can become a liveryman but that is not a hard rule and I was therefore surprised when I received a letter in early 2001, less than four years after joining, inviting me to become one. I quickly accepted this offer which I regarded as an honour and a privilege. I first had to go through a delightful ceremony to be granted the freedom of the City of London and then, after I had paid what is called the 'livery fine', I was 'clothed' by the then master, Michael Grayburn, as a liveryman at the 2001 Trophies and Awards Banquet at the Guildhall. Almost immediately, I received separate telephone calls from, I recall, three past masters, Captain Rod Fulton, Captain Clive Elton and Captain Chris Hodgkinson, and a then warden who would shortly become master, Duncan Simpson, suggesting that, now that I was entitled, I should put my name forward for the annual competition to become an assistant of the court. Up to that point, I had not considered the subject but I did so on their advice and was elected to become an assistant in March 2002. Then, less than two years later, it was suggested to me, again through telephone calls, that I might put my name forward for the 2004 competition for the election of a new warden. Every year, a new warden is elected by all voting members of the court. Again, I was deeply honoured to be elected and I knew that all being well I was now on a completely new pathway to become master of the Air Pilots. The lead-in time is long but necessary, there is a lot to learn. I first served for a year as junior warden, then a year as middle warden, a year as senior warden and, finally, a year as master-elect before I was installed as 'master' in March 2008, only just over ten years after I had joined the company. My progress since joining had been rapid and I would never have predicted that I would become master in such a short time. It was a great honour and a privilege to become master and I regarded the elevation as the pinnacle in my long career in aviation. It was also a position that itself opened up many new doors in my life.

My year as master was a very special year in every respect. Not only was I in the senior position within the Air Pilots, I was now also one of a total of 108 masters of the various livery companies. There were many opportunities to get to know my fellow masters from other livery companies, at individual livery company functions, at the two annual elections, respectively, for the sheriffs and the lord mayor. Also, in June 2008, a weekend get together was held in Shropshire, known as the 'Ironbridge' weekend, which was attended by most masters. Essentially, this was a masters' bonding event and we toured Ironbridge and other locations and sat down to black tie dinners on both the Friday and Saturday nights. Also, on the Sunday, we had a meeting to decide on plans for a past masters' association for our year. From that meeting emerged the name of my past masters' association, 'The After Eights', an association that has thrived ever since and of which I am currently a committee member.

During my year as master I chaired many meetings, monthly of the executive committee, bi-monthly of the court, those associated with a strategic review which took place in my year as master and other meetings associated with day-to-day activities. I hosted every function that took place, and there were many, and I was invited to many functions with other livery companies. I went on all of the many visits that took place including two overseas visits lasting up to a week, one to Florida, USA, and to Cyprus. The Florida visit was mainly to tour the Cape Kennedy Space Center and the one to Cyprus to visit the Red Arrows during their final work-up for the display season. These were both memorable occasions. I also visited Canada twice and South Africa at least three times. These trips were mainly associated with a stated aim for my year, outlined in my speech at the installation supper after I had been 'installed' as master, when I stated that I would set in hand the setting-up of new regions in both countries. I was successful in Canada and a new region had been created before I handed over the reins of being master to my successor. However, I was less successful in South Africa even though there was a long aviation history linking the UK with that country. The roots of the reason for both success and delay in these two missions were the same, in Canada I had quickly found someone to be the champion (chairman) of the new region, but no champion could be found in South Africa even though there was considerable support. However, another event worthy of mention did take place in South Africa.

The year 2008 marked the 70th anniversary of one of the longest-standing records in aviation; the time taken to fly from London to Cape Town and back to London in a single-engine aircraft. The record was held by a great name in aviation, Alex Henshaw. My intention had been to hold a special dinner in London followed by another special dinner in Cape Town to celebrate this milestone. In the end, it was decided not to hold a dinner in London but the one planned for Cape Town did take place in January 2009 and was a great success. It was held in the officers' mess at the South African Air Force base at Ysterplaat, near Cape Town, and it was attended by many dignitaries from both the UK and South Africa, from all walks of aviation. It was a truly memorable occasion. I knew the chairman of Emirates Airlines at the time and Emirates very kindly provided a number of free tickets that enabled some people to attend who might not have otherwise been able to do so.

The guests of honour were both holders of the world land speed record, Richard Noble, a former holder, and Wing Commander Andy Green, the current record holder. Andy Green is the only man to have gone supersonic on land and his record speed still stands at 763 mph. However, Richard, as the project manager, and Andy, as the planned driver, were intending then, and are still hoping today, to take the record to 1,000 mph in a car called 'Bloodhound', and at a location which has already been identified in the Western Cape in South Africa. The main organiser of the dinner in Cape Town, Skip Margetts, a great chap who runs his own aviation film company in the Cape, is also now their project manager for the site of the record attempt in South Africa. I was very sorry that we did not have greater success with attempts to establish a region in South Africa but I was delighted with the success of the Alex Henshaw dinner and we had a lot of fun during our visits to South Africa to organise the event. On these visits I was accompanied by the excellent clerk (chief executive) of the Air Pilots, Paul Tacon, and by another assistant who also became master several years later, His Honour Judge Tudor Owen. We stayed at a lovely place in the country, at Noordhoek, about 30 minutes from Cape Town, called the Wild Rose. Suffice to say, we had a lot of fun and burnt the candle at every end.

Undoubtedly, however, the highlight of my year as master, and the highlight of the year for every master of the Air Pilots, was 'The Masters Tour of the Regions', Canada (now a part of the North American region), New Zealand, Australia and Hong Kong. This tour effectively takes you around the world, it certainly did in my case which, as it turned out, also carried some twists and turns. About two weeks before I was due to commence my tour, accompanied by my wife, we were attending a dinner at Peterhouse College, Cambridge at which Sir Michael Marshall, the chairman of a well-known, privately owned, aviation company, Marshalls of Cambridge, presented the Air Pilots with a new silver 'Loving Cup' in memory of his father, Sir Arthur Marshall, a previous chairman of the same family company, also very well-known in aviation circles and who had recently died aged 103. After returning to our hotel we spent a little more time at the bar and people gradually disappeared to bed and there were just three of us left. Unfortunately, I fell asleep whilst sitting on a stool at the bar and fell off and broke my wrist. Now this event was not in my plans and caused me (and Tina!) some difficulty during the tour because I had planned to do quite a lot of flying and play a lot of golf. Oh dear! The next day Tina drove us back to Berkshire where I first had my wrist x-rayed which confirmed a clean break and then we had to go to the hospital at Frimley Park in Berkshire where I was given laughing gas whilst the bone was manipulated back into place and I was put in plaster. Unfortunately, when I went for my check-up the next week the wrist wasn't quite set in the right place and I ended up in hospital for a night to have an operation to pin the bone in place. This was successfully done but I was worried because my tour was due to start in little more than a week and I did not want to be delayed. Fortunately, we departed on time but I don't think Tina was over-impressed with me because she had to drag my suitcase around as well as hers and she also had to help me with things like getting dressed. It certainly added to the experience.

My masters tour lasted for about seven weeks. We first flew to Washington accompanied by our good friends, Air Marshal Cliff and Caroline Spink. Cliff also became master of the Air Pilots a few years later. The tour also started on a high when the four of us were upgraded to first class on our British Airways flight from Heathrow. Whilst in Washington for several days I gave two talks and we visited the White House for a specially arranged VIP tour. The experience of seeing the Oval Office left an impression on me which I am reminded about often when seeing the news from America because I can visualise exactly the location and size of the room itself. From Washington,

Cliff and Caroline returned to the UK whilst Tina and I flew to Vancouver to visit the newest region. We stayed with, and were hosted by throughout, the chairman of the Canadian region, John Burley, and his lovely wife, Liz. From Vancouver we flew to Auckland, New Zealand, via San Francisco. We had a super week in New Zealand where we stayed with Allan and Lyn Boyce. Allan is an ex-Royal New Zealand Air Force pilot and was now a senior captain with Air New Zealand. Our week was a busy one and, whilst we spent most of the time in the vicinity of Auckland, we also visited Wellington where I hosted a cocktail party at which I was delighted to see a number of my ex-RAF colleagues. They were now either living or working in New Zealand. We then flew to Melbourne, to commence a two-week visit to Australia. This was a very busy two weeks and we visited many different locations and organisations in and around Brisbane, Melbourne, Adelaide and Sydney.

My broken wrist came out of plaster whilst we were in Adelaide and I even managed to do some flying including an interesting one in a seaplane whilst in Sydney. After a memorable and action-packed two weeks it was time once again to leave Australia and fly to Hong Kong for a final and again action-packed visit. Throughout all these trips we met some very interesting and important people, we had a number of meetings with government departments, and we enjoyed many social activities where I invariably had to speak for my supper, a task that I welcomed and enjoyed. I did manage to fly on a number of occasions but I was unable to play the golf that I had planned which was a pity. After Hong Kong we flew to Dubai for a few days to visit our eldest daughter, Lisa, who was running her own headhunting business. From there we flew back to the UK and home in time for all the pre-Christmas festivities, the end of a trip never to be forgotten.

My year as master ended in March 2009, it had been a momentous and wonderful experience and it most certainly was the pinnacle of my aviation career. I remain to this day very involved with the Honourable Company of Air Pilots and from 2009 to 2019 I also chaired the prestigious trophies and awards committee, a task that gave me great pleasure. I had an excellent and very high-profile committee to help make the decisions and it was so satisfying to read all the citations of achievement in the aviation world and to see the recipients acclaimed at the annual banquet. There is one that I will never forget and that was the banquet, in I think it was 2005, when the first man to walk on the moon, Neil Armstrong, was to receive the major award, the Award of Honour, for his lifetime achievements. I had the enviable task of being his host for the evening and sitting next to him at the dinner, which was something very special. He was the nicest person one could ever meet, very unassuming, just a gracious man. The 700 other diners were all in awe of this special occasion.

Other things which I will also remember were the occasions on which I had the honour to meet royalty. Prince Andrew was the grand master of the Air Pilots and, when I was master, I had at least two audiences with him at Buckingham Palace. Prince Philip was the patron and he too I met on a number of occasions either at Buckingham Palace or at Air Pilots functions. And finally, Tina and I attended a royal garden party at Buckingham Palace and we were honoured to be singled out to meet Her Majesty the Queen. We must have spent at least three or four minutes talking with Her Majesty, another memorable event. I think, and know, that the master-elect, and my successor as master, Rear Admiral Colin Cooke-Priest, an exceptional man and officer, and who was the chief gentleman usher to the Queen at the time, had been instrumental in making this happen. Thank you, Colin!

I said at the start of this chapter that my involvement with the Air Pilots has had a significant effect on my life since joining the company and it has. I have met so many people that I would not otherwise have met and done things that I would not have had the chance to do. It has also put my name in lights on occasions and it has opened doors that have given me additional opportunities away from the Air Pilots. These openings have themselves given me a lot of satisfaction, in so many different directions. Joining the Air Pilots was one of the best decisions that I have made in my life.

CHAPTER 17
THE ROYAL AIR FORCE CLUB

The Royal Air Force Club is situated in Piccadilly, London and is a magnificent place. The Royal Air Force was formed in 1918, the last year of World War I, when the Royal Flying Corps and the Royal Naval Air Service combined and formed the RAF. That same year, Lord Cowdray provided the initial funds for a Royal Air Force Club and the search for premises led to the selection and purchase of the present site of the club on 31st October 1918. At the time it was the site of the Ladies Lyceum Club, a tavern called 'The Running Horse' and stables on the adjacent Old Park Lane. Lord Cowdray then provided further funding to convert the site into the RAF Club. The club was formally opened by the Duke of York in March 1922. Over the years it has further developed and is now one of the most sought-after and prestigious clubs in London. The membership numbers almost 25,000, there are now 110 bedrooms and there are a number of banqueting rooms of varying sizes. Uniquely, the club has preserved the memory of the Running Horse Tavern and this is one of the most popular venues in the club for some relaxing libation.

I have been a member of the RAF Club since I joined the RAF in 1965 and, from 2009 until December 2018 I was a trustee on the board of trustees. Also, for almost seven years of that time I was the vice chairman, a position which I hugely enjoyed and which gave me great satisfaction. Becoming a trustee followed very neatly on from my year as master of the Honourable Company of Air Pilots and it enabled me to continue what I like doing most, meeting and working with people and, of course, the RAF Club is also all about aviation, my great love. During my time as a trustee I was involved in a lot of development within the club. The biggest complaint from members was that it was sometimes difficult to book rooms when required and we knew that we had to find a way of providing more bedrooms. At the time, we had 93 bedrooms and we looked at a number of options. Eventually, after a lot of consideration, and discussion, we decided to build a new wing which would provide an additional 17 bedrooms to take the number to 110, plus a new fitness centre and business suite. Unfortunately, the bedrooms were built at the expense of two squash courts which, if they remained, were going to need a lot of expenditure on maintenance. Also, the courts were extremely under-utilised and, quite frankly, there was no business case for their retention. I was sad to see them go, particularly as I had always been a squash player, but the decision that we made as a board of trustees was the best and only sensible decision to make.

The highlight of my time as vice chairman was probably the opportunity to be so deeply involved with the club's centenary celebrations in 2018. There were special dinners to attend, I hosted a magnificent centenary summer ball and the all-round celebrations that took place on 31st October. However, the highlight has to be the visit of Her Majesty the Queen, the patron of the club, on 17th October 2018. She attended a reception in her honour and she formally opened the new wing, unveiled a new stained-glass window to commemorate 100 years of achievement by women in the RAF, and unveiled the portrait of herself that we had specially commissioned and which was painted by the portrait artist, Ben Sullivan. I also hosted two royal receptions held in St James Palace, the first attended by the Countess of Wessex and the second by Princess Eugenie. 2018 was a very special year in the history of the RAF Club and yet another year impressed on my memory.

As vice chairman I worked closely with the chief executive and club secretary and that was another aspect of the job which I very much liked. When I became vice chairman, the club secretary was Peter Owen who eventually retired from the post in 2015 after 24 years in situ. He remains a good friend. His successor was Miles Pooley and he too has done, and continues to do, an excellent job, taking the club to the next level since he took up the appointment. I was particularly pleased to see the success of Miles because I was chairman of the selection committee that recommended his appointment. I must also make a special mention of Kathryn Cooper, the club manager and the longest-serving member of the staff. I had long recognised her value to the club and I could see that she was like a rock to the senior management and trustees. In fact, so much so was that the case that one of the criteria that we laid down in our search for the new chief executive and club secretary was that we had to be confident that the new incumbent would have a good working relationship with Kathryn. That has certainly proved to be the case. I always took a great interest in the staff of the club and made sure that I got to know them well, an effort that, in my view, paid, and continues to pay, rich dividends. The club staff have always been a mainly happy group and I have greatly enjoyed an excellent working relationship, they are all special people.

As with any large organisation, there were always problems to resolve and I found myself involved with a number of these situations. In many ways, my position had similar responsibilities to those when I had been station commander of RAF Leeming. There were undoubted challenges but then I have always liked to have challenges.

I have always had an interest in art. I had won the art prize on a number of occasions at school and I had studied art for a year at university. It is also a dormant hobby of mine at home and I have been threatening to start painting again for many years. My threats have become a bit of a standing joke with my family who have listened to me postulating but have yet to see any action. I still fully intend to return to painting, I have all the equipment needed to paint, I simply have not had the time up until now. However, I now have a studio at home and so family, watch this space! I mention this here because the RAF Club possesses a very impressive collection of aviation paintings and squadron badges, and I sit on the arts committee. I greatly value my involvement with the art of the club and I have had considerable enjoyment from my part in the making of some very important decisions about the art. The collection of squadron badges is unique and the only such collection anywhere in the world. All of the several hundred squadron badges displayed in the club are original badges from the College of Arms. It is also interesting to see how members of the club react when paintings are moved to new locations, you can always be certain that someone will make a comment. There is nothing that seems to generate more controversy than art.

My role as vice chairman was, arguably, one of the most important roles in the RAF Club, especially so since the chairman was always a senior serving RAF officer with a busy full-time job and who rarely served as chairman for longer than a couple of years. In my role I was very much the continuity person who was able to spend more time involved with the day-to-day business of the club. I loved the job.

I feel that I achieved much during my time as a trustee and vice chairman but in particular I will remember the part that I played in the following aspects, events or decisions:

- The building of the centenary wing, and in particular the part that I played in arranging for the RAF Benevolent Fund to sponsor the new fitness centre, and Marshalls of Cambridge to sponsor the new business suite.

- The 2018 centenary celebrations.

• The development of art policy and the arrangements for the display of the squadron badges. This is very much an on-going task. However, over the last five or six years, I am particularly proud to have been involved in the development of an 'acquisition and disposal policy', the development of a proper plan for the display of squadron badges, and the categorisation of all paintings and artefacts. These categories range from category one to four where categories one and two relate to the items which the club would wish to retain at all costs, and where category four is an indication that the club would be prepared to offload items, subject to history. I was also actively involved with the paintings commissioned by the last two presidents of the RAF Club, Air Chief Marshal Sir Peter Squire, a former chief of the Air Staff, and Air Marshal Sir David Walker, a former head of the Royal Household. I should add, however, that it was the two presidents who had the final say on the artist selected to do the relevant painting. These portraits now hang in the President's Room at the RAF Club. There are many other art decisions in which I have had a direct influence, some described below. I am also very proud of the way in which the arts committee has developed since the turn of the century in year 2000. The art of the RAF Club is more than a unique selling point for the club, it defines the character and prestige of the club itself.

• The commissioning of a triptych to commemorate the demise of military search and rescue, and unveiled by HRH Prince Andrew, Duke of York, in March 2015. Search and rescue, and air-sea rescue have, since World War II, played a vital part in RAF history and there are many aircrew, both RAF and other services, who owe their lives to this capability and branch of the RAF.

• Commissioning the artist Tim O'Brien to produce excellent new art that can be seen in the dining room. Each painting, and there are many, tells a story about the RAF.

• Arranging for a No. 23 Squadron triptych to be displayed in the club. This is a superb triptych, painted by a former RAF Lightning pilot, Chris Stone, and an example of the type of problem created through the standing-down of front-line RAF squadrons, and the downsizing in the size of the RAF. Paintings and artefacts suddenly find themselves without a home and I am delighted, in this case, to have been able to help, and in the process work closely with Air Chief Marshal Sir William Wratten, one of my past commanders, himself an ex-officer commanding of No. 23 Squadron, and one whom I greatly respect.

• The renaming and opening of the Churchill Bar which had previously been known as the 'Club Main Bar'. The opening was attended by descendants of Sir Winston Churchill, Lord Trenchard, and General Jan Smuts. It was a very special, and appropriate, event. Sir Winston Churchill was himself an honorary air commodore and the club possesses a very fine painting of Churchill in air commodore uniform. This painting now, appropriately, hangs in the Churchill Bar and is the focal point of attention. I played a very major part in all these decisions. I should add that, since the Churchill Bar was named, the club has also been presented with a unique violin made from Churchill's cigar boxes. The violin has been played by the renowned musician, Yehudi Menuhin, and is displayed in the Churchill Bar together with a Churchill cigar and a bust of the great man. These artefacts were presented by a personal friend, Gerry O'Brien, who for over 30 years had been the landlord of the 'unique' Churchill Arms pub in Kensington Church Street in London.

• The renaming of the Battle of Britain Suite, previously known as the 'Millenium Suite', and which also incorporates the Spitfire and Hurricane Rooms. As the son of a Battle of Britain pilot, I considered that this famous battle which, in many ways, defined the RAF as a fighting service, should be more publicly commemorated within the RAF Club. I make no apology for claiming that the original proposal came directly from me whilst vice chairman, recognising, of course, that other committees and the board of trustees were all involved in making the final, appropriate, decision.

• The selection of the new chief executive officer and club secretary, Miles Pooley, in 2015. This was a time-consuming procedure. The previous incumbent, Peter Owen, had been in post for 24 years and there was little historical paperwork to help guide the process. Also, the recruitment process had changed greatly over the years. Effectively, I had to ensure that the club adhered to modern recruitment process and this meant a lot of hard work in putting in hand the correct procedures and paperwork. The result was well worth the effort and the club is reaping the benefit.

• The excellent relationship that I had with the club management and staff, and, also, with the membership at large. This relationship is never a given and requires time, effort and commitment. It was well worth all of those and I continue to enjoy an excellent relationship with all three elements now that I am a past vice chairman.

I think readers will understand that I will always hold very fond memories of my time involved with the RAF Club, as both a member for over 50 years, a trustee for ten years, and vice chairman for seven years. The RAF Club feels very much a part of ME.

CHAPTER 18
MY MANY OTHER INTERESTS AND ACTIVITIES

I have always been a 'can do' man and I have always liked being busy but even I will admit that for the last ten years or so I have taken on too much and at the expense of spare time and, as I have discovered, time on the golf course. I say to people, "I like doing a lot and I don't do anything these days that I do not like doing". True words but I did take on too much. Anyway, in this chapter I want to recall details of my interests and activities that I have not covered elsewhere in this book.

In Command Ltd

In Command is a company that, together with my business partners, Jan Dawson, and Peter Scoffham, I formed back in 2010. Jan had previously run her own PR company and also been elected Business Woman of the Year for the East of England and Peter was a good friend from my RAF days, a well-known raconteur and good chap. Our primary aim was to set up a company which would bring the military and business worlds closer together and, importantly, make the business world more aware of the excellence and quality of the military person and the capabilities that they could offer. We formed the company and appointed a board which included the three of us plus a high-flying American, Alex Adamopoulis, who ran his own fast-developing company, and two retired senior military officers, Rear Admiral Simon Williams, a Royal Navy submariner and Air Vice-Marshal Brian Bates.

The company developed quickly, with hindsight too quickly. Initially, we had concentrated on providing ex-military speakers under an arm of the company called Speakers in Command. However, the company quickly grew and three new departments of the business were created. Leaders in Command was created to provide training for 15 or more different areas of expertise including subjects such as leadership, human performance, cyber security, media and PR to name but some. To provide this training, we had recruited on to our books many military experts who were used on an 'as required basis' rather than being direct employees. We all had a very significant number of contacts and so it was not difficult to find the people that we wanted. Next, we set up Events in Command which, again, was planned to use our level of contacts, contacts that we knew others could not reach, to create a number of unique offerings of events. Also, to help us, we had agents in various overseas countries, again mainly people who we already knew. As it transpired, this has probably been our most successful department and a number of influential people, especially from overseas countries such as Canada, have enjoyed visits to the UK and experiences that they probably thought were never possible. Our final department was titled Recruitment in Command and, initially, this was set up simply to deal with very special recruitment requirements involving ex-military personnel, and because we again had the necessary contacts.

In Command remains in existence and we still have the capability to meet almost any request but I will be honest, in recent times we have really been concentrating on a new and very interesting, and exciting, venture, Battle of Britain Tours.

Creating and running In Command has been great fun but it has also been a great challenge for a number of reasons. First and foremost, all three of us involved had many other interests and, therefore, none of us was in a position to devote fully the amount of time needed to develop and, in particular, market the company. Also, we only had limited funds and this again prevented us from spending the amount of money that was probably required on the marketing front. And finally, Peter was living in Cornwall and coming to London more or less on an as required basis. He had other responsibilities in Cornwall, both family and local, and he therefore had to end his involvement. This was a pity because he brought a lot to the company, he always had plenty of ideas and, moreover, he was very good social company. We miss his presence. All this has meant that In Command has probably been run more as a hobby than anything else but the capability remains and, who knows, it could suddenly take off, if or when someone shows greater interest.

Battle of Britain Tours

Battle of Britain Tours, which is run, at present, as a further department within In Command, is the direction in which our time has been focused over the last few years and, we believe, has great potential. So how did this interest develop?

As the reader now knows, my father was a Battle of Britain pilot and he and all the Battle of Britain pilots were my heroes as a youngster. He and they are still my heroes today and their way of life, as I understood it, has driven me throughout my career. I can well remember my father saying to me, on a regular basis, "Son, work hard; play hard". I have, all my life! I am passionate about the Battle of Britain and I am passionate that everyone should be made fully cognisant of that time in 1940 and what it meant for the United Kingdom. But time moves on and I worry that, as the years go by, our descendants won't be taught about this very important part of our history.

Also, I was always aware of the separate battlefield tours that took place. People talked a lot about these tours and they were available in many places but, in particular, in France and South Africa. I had never heard anyone talk about Battle of Britain tours and I asked myself 'Why?' and started to investigate. I discovered that, whilst there were locally run tours in various places, the possibility and/or opportunity to go on a 'nationally marketed' tour of important Battle of Britain facilities and sites was seemingly non-existent. That was how our Battle of Britain tours initiative was launched.

There are many important Battle of Britain locations in the east and southeast of England and a number of them have in recent years had millions of pounds spent on facilities. We visited many of these locations to see for ourselves what had been done, and it is impressive. At what was the headquarters of Fighter Command during the battle, Bentley Priory, an excellent Battle of Britain museum has been created which is a must to visit. Many millions of pounds have been spent on developing the museum. At the site of the Battle of Britain operations bunker at Uxbridge, millions of pounds have been spent on building a visitor centre near the entrance to the bunker. Visitors to the bunker are able to see what the operations room looked like on 15th September 1940, known as Battle of Britain Day. Millions of pounds have been spent on facilities at Biggin Hill in Kent and also on the excellent new 'Wing' at the site on the White Cliffs, Capel-le-Ferne where a Battle of Britain memorial is located and which is the home of the Battle of Britain Memorial Trust. There, they also have what is known as 'the Scramble Experience' which is a first-class and most memorable experience to visit. In fact, I have gone on record as saying that it should be compulsory that everyone in the UK who possesses a British passport should visit the site at least once in their lifetime, the earlier the better. As Sir Winston Churchill said, "They will not be forgotten", words that I would only echo. There is so much to see and I have vowed that, as long as I am in this world, I will do all possible to preserve the names of those who were called 'The Few', and to educate others on the history of the Battle of Britain. As I write these words in 2019, I am conscious that there are now only three Battle of Britain pilots still living and that soon there will be none. I owe it to my father and those brave men to preserve their names and achievements.

Through both In Command and Battle of Britain Tours, we have met a lot of new people and had some fascinating encounters and experiences, very rewarding in human terms it has been too, and, of course, it has all been great fun. My work associated with the Battle of Britain is ongoing and I am very hopeful that our initiative will gain traction, there is certainly a lot of interest in the UK and from around the world.

There are also other things that I do in my life which one could say have a connection with the Battle of Britain, as will become apparent in the next paragraphs.

Air Displays

I have had a long association with air displays, from being a display pilot when flying in the RAF to then becoming involved with the supervision of air displays. This dates back to 1991 when I was station commander at RAF Leeming and was responsible for the selection of the Tornado F3 display pilot and the work-up and supervision of all display practices. Then, in the mid-1990s, when I was the RAF's Inspector of Flight Safety, I had an even deeper involvement in a number of ways. First, it was a time when flying control committees (FCC) were being introduced to help supervise air displays. Through my inspectorate, we ran the first courses for those destined to sit on these committees. Also, I was invited to become a member of the flying control committee for the Royal International Air Tattoo (RIAT) at Fairford, Gloucestershire. This was a very senior and influential committee and there were some great characters who were members of the committee, like Brian 'Trubby' Trubshaw, the well-known Concorde test pilot. I spent 19 very happy years on the RIAT FCC and it was a great experience. I thoroughly enjoyed the camaraderie on the FCC which comprised eight members from both military and civil aviation. There was work to do but there was also time for play. The social highlight for me was always our attendance at the gala dinner on the Friday night of the RIAT weekend, a very special occasion every year.

My involvement with RIAT also led to my participation in other air displays, notably the Farnborough International Air Display which takes place every two years. In the mid-1990s Farnborough was still an MoD-owned airfield but the show was a civil air display. It was realised that there was no military representation on the Farnborough FCC, on which the members were all test pilots, and the Secretary of State requested RAF representation. As Inspector of Flight Safety, and because of my involvement with RIAT, I was perfectly placed and was delighted to be invited to join the team, supposedly for only one air display because by the next one the airfield would no longer be MoD-owned. Some 24 years later and I am still involved and there are now two non-test pilot members of the FCC, myself and my good friend, Les Garside-Beattie, a Harrier pilot, with whom I had worked on the RIAT FCC and who used to be manager of the Red Arrows.

Around 1998, I was invited to join the FCC at the Imperial War Museum airfield, Duxford, and that began a 20-year association, initially as a member of the FCC and then for 15 years as chairman before I handed over to my deputy, Al Lockwood, at the end of the 2018 air display season. However, I remain involved with Duxford as the chairman of another committee that oversees all operations at Duxford and reports to the IWM board of trustees in London through their audit board. Anyone who knows Duxford will know that it is a World War II Battle of Britain airfield and to this day remains mainly unspoilt. It is a very special place in so many ways, there is so much to see and do there and, most importantly, it is the home of the 'warbirds' in the UK. Spitfires, Hurricanes and other warbird aircraft can always be seen there. It is not uncommon at the annual September Battle of Britain air display to see participating in excess of 20 Spitfires and also a number of Hurricanes. There are three two-day air shows each year, all slightly different but involving some great aircraft. Being in charge of the FCC has been a rewarding experience and has enabled me and my team to develop an excellent relationship with the pilot community, many of them with names of legendary status. The FCC was arguably the best in the UK and included some well-known names in the air display and wider aviation world: Roger Beazley, Geoff Brindle, Tom Eeles, Al Lockwood, Andy Stewart, Jim Jewell, Mike Wood, Dave Evans, Sam Whatmough, Gabriel Barton, Shaun Wildey, Tom Boyle and Paul Farmer to name but some who served on the FCC in my time. I appreciated their support and we operated well as a team, both at work and play, in true Battle of Britain style. Some of the banter was outstanding, particularly since at least five of us had been Lightning pilots and there was always a lot of WIWOL talk. That would always get Andy Stewart into banter mode.

My involvement with air displays continued to grow. I was invited to join a number of other FCCs and I also became more involved as a flying display director (FDD). I now run, on an annual basis, a number of displays in my FDD capacity. The jewel in my crown is the Newcastle (Northern Ireland) Festival of Flight Air Display, a very beautiful venue. One other air display venture which gives me special pleasure is what has become my annual trip to the island of Jersey for the Jersey International Air Display. In I think it must have been 2012, the organiser of the Jersey IAD, Mike Higgins, invited me to carry out an audit of the air display. I did this and submitted my report and ever since I have been invited to attend each year in much the same capacity.

I must also make mention of another special air display for which I was the flying display director in 2018, a two-day 'Heroes at Highclere' air display which was held at Highclere Castle, the home of Lord and Lady Carnarvon. Highclere Castle has become particularly well known in recent years because it was where the television series 'Downton Abbey' was filmed. It was an excellent site to hold an air display and it was a great pleasure to meet and work with Lord and Lady Carnarvon and their staff. Lady Carnarvon, who is a very dynamic lady with boundless enthusiasm and energy, project managed the event which included many other attractions in addition to the air display. My own flying display team included Steve Bohill-Smith, a retired Concorde pilot and George Bacon who is very well known in both army aviation and air display circles. Highclere 2018 was a memorable experience.

Obviously, the tragic accident that occurred during the 2016 Shoreham Air Display and which claimed the lives of 11 innocent civilians, has had a major effect on events in the UK and the aftermath continues. However, I still believe that air displays will take place for the foreseeable future, albeit that rules and regulations may continue to be further refined.

Historic Aircraft Association

The Historic Aircraft Association, known affectionately as the HAA, was formed in 1979 to look after the interests of the historic aircraft community. The main responsibility was the provision of display authorisations for that community to participate in air displays. I was initially invited to become chairman of the HAA and then for the six years up until April 2019 to be the president. The HAA is another organisation which can and should be very influential, it is, and I have very much enjoyed my association which continues. I handed over as president, in April 2019, to Sir Gerald 'Biggles' Howarth, a good friend of many years standing who is a well-known ex-Member of Parliament with a deep interest in aviation. I can think of no-one better to fill my shoes.

The HAA is an organisation which links with my other interests and has again given me much satisfaction. I have met and worked with some excellent people from the industry – aircrew and engineers, aircraft owners, industry regulators and others. There have been a number of major issues to deal with and I always felt that we owed it to the outstanding group of people who were the founding members of the HAA, famous aviators like Duncan Simpson, Darryl Stinton, Peter Thorne and Desmond Penrose to name a few, to do our best to help preserve and look after the industry.

General Aviation Safety Council

In 2011 I was approached by the then chairman of the General Aviation Safety Council (GASCo), Gerald Hackemer, to see if I was interested in having my name put forward to take over from him as chairman of that organisation. At the time, I already had a lot on my plate but aviation safety has always attracted my interest, and I knew that this was an opportunity that I would have regretted if I had turned it down. After several months of deep thinking, I accepted the offer. I always knew that I would, and I was delighted when the board of GASCo approved my appointment. I served six years as chairman of GASCo, working with a small but excellent team. Especially worthy of mention are Mike O'Donaghue, the chief executive, and Penny Gould, the administrator, both of whom have made an invaluable contribution to the organisation.

I was very proud of my association with GASCo and the overall achievements of the organisation. Chairing meetings of the council brought it home to me just how broad a parish the general aviation sector was, from business jets to aerobatics, from gliding to microlights and parachuting, there were over 40 members of the GASCo Council. Each representative at council meetings was there to represent their specific corner of the aviation world. I found it fascinating to learn about each and every organisation and to hear about their respective successes and concerns about aviation safety. The experience has broadened my mind and made me much more aware about the world of general aviation. GASCo is a very successful organisation and excellent value for money, and in particular as far as the Civil Aviation Authority (CAA) was concerned. On behalf of the CAA, GASCo was contracted to run a number of general aviation safety evenings each year and also regular airspace infringement awareness courses. In both these cases the achievements were usually well in excess of the contractual requirement. To steer the policy direction of GASCo, I chaired an excellent group of well-known aviation leaders and, overall, my time at the head of GASCo was a very satisfying experience. In July 2018, I handed over to another luminary in the aviation world, Professor Mike Bagshaw who has just about the most impressive CV that I have ever read – there would seem to be nothing that he hasn't done.

International Air Cadets Training Organisation

I was pleased to be invited to become a trustee of the International Air Cadets Training (IACT) organisation and then to become chairman of a very impressive board of trustees. I believe strongly in the RAF Air Cadets Organisation with whom, over the years, I have had growing contact and here was an opportunity to develop similar organisations in other countries. Without going into detail, suffice to say that there has been a lot of interest from many countries and a number of initiatives have been launched over the years. The difficulty has always been converting interest into action and negotiations can take many years. Also, there is always a need for government involvement. A change in policy direction or leadership, also the availability of funds, can often deny success. As I write these words, I am conscious of ongoing discussions with a number of countries and I strongly believe that there are excellent opportunities to help develop the youth of other nations and to export our own success with the RAF Air Cadets Organisation.

Air Search UK

Air Search UK is an organisation about which few are aware but it provides a very useful service in the field of air investigations, as the name would suggest. All those involved are volunteers. They use their own aircraft and helicopters to carry out the various searches that are requested and the organisation works closely with the police, mainly in the south-east. Tasks are multi-varied but often involve the search for people and the general policing of the coast and shoreline for illegal activities.

Air Search UK was set up by Peter Adams, Lord Abbotts-Hay, and he runs a very useful body full of enthusiastic aviators. I first came into contact with Air Search UK when I was invited to speak at one of their annual dinners. The then-president of Air Search UK was none other than the legendary test pilot Eric 'Winkle' Brown and I felt deeply honoured when I was invited to succeed him as president, a role that I hold to this day.

CHIRP

For about 15 years I was a trustee of the Confidential Human Incident Reporting Programme (CHIRP), a charity which oversees the running of a confidential reporting programme for aviation and maritime matters. My involvement in CHIRP went back to my time as the RAF's Inspector of Flight Safety when I ran a separate confidential reporting system known as CONDOR. The two systems were run in different ways but the aims were the same, the protection of the confidentiality of individuals, to learn about issues and the resolution of problems. It was like a large window to the issues across the aviation sector in the UK. CHIRP provided a very useful and productive forum in terms of the provision of solutions. The charity was an important contributor to overall aviation safety. During my time with CHIRP I was also privileged to have the opportunity to travel to Australia and to give a presentation on confidential reporting at the 2009 Safe Skies Conference in Canberra.

Aviation Skills Partnership

Aviation Skills Partnership (ASP) was founded by Simon Witts and was another organisation with which, as soon as I had been briefed on future plans, I knew that I wanted to be involved. ASP was founded with the prime intention of preserving the future of aviation in the UK and to develop an interest in aviation in the young, and from an early age. The intention was to build about 20 international aviation academies all over the UK and to train people in a number of aviation skills – piloting, engineering, air traffic control, operations and simulation to name some of the available areas of expertise. The first academy, a very impressive place, has already been built and opened at Norwich airport and a number of other academies are at varying stages of the planning process. A close relationship has been developed with academia, industry and the RAF. The RAF Air Cadets Organisation is already making use of facilities. This is a very exciting venture and, all being well, should help to develop and increase interest in aviation. Heritage also plays an important part in future plans and that is the main area where I have been asked to take an interest and devote time. I am delighted to do just that.

My Hobbies

Not including my overall interest in sport, with everything that I do in my busy life there has been little time to spend on my quoted main hobbies, stamp collecting and painting, but I hope that both will reap the benefit of my time as I step down from my various responsibilities.

I have a very large collection of stamps and this has been an 'on and off' interest for most of my life ever since my father helped develop this interest in my early years. I started by collecting world stamps before I then began to concentrate first on South Africa and Great Britain and then just Great Britain. In recent years, I have further refined my main interest in stamps to those issued during the reign of Queen Victoria. My stamps tend to appear over the Christmas break and my collection gives me a lot of pleasure. My family can't understand how I can get pleasure from moving stamps around in my albums.

My other main hobby is art and painting although the painting side is somewhat dormant at present. My interest in painting goes back to my school days when I won the art prize on a number of occasions. I then studied art for a year at university and at one stage I had a portfolio of about 150 paintings that I had done. My main painting interest is in land and seascapes and abstract art. Watch this space!

My Growing Family

Having written all of the above, I must finish by saying that nothing is more important than my family, my wife, Tina, my three children, Lisa, Jenny and Ian, and now my two very beautiful granddaughters, Maisie, now aged four and Annabelle, aged two. They all give Tina and I great pleasure and, in saying all this, I also recognise the considerable part played by Jenny's husband, Andy, in her and our lives.

Lisa, a partner in a headhunting firm, currently lives in New York but spends much time in the UK as well, and so we do see a lot of her. Jenny lives nearby in Bracknell and Ian even closer in Sandhurst and so we feel very lucky that we see a lot of two of our children and our granddaughters. Tina and I live in the village of Crowthorne in Berkshire and also own a villa in Croatia where the family, both together and individually, have enjoyed some pleasant holidays over the years, with families and friends.

EPILOGUE
REFLECTIONS

As I reach my final words in this book, I find myself reflecting on the reasons why I decided to write it in the first place, and also some things that I know that I have not yet discussed.

First, however, let me explain the reasons for writing the book, which are many. Over the years, a lot of people have asked me when I was going to write my memoirs to which my answer was always 'in due course'. On reflection, I knew that I had had a very varied career and that there was much that was worth recording for others to read. So I sat down about ten years ago and drew up a structure for the book. However, I decided to go no further until I had first sought the views of a publisher. In due course, about six or seven years ago now, I met a person who was both an editor and publisher. I gave him my book structure to consider over a weekend and he came back to me on the Monday saying that he thought the structure was brilliant and that he would write the book for me. I said, "You have got yourself a job, I am just a fighter pilot and I am not over keen on writing the book myself". There followed many meetings, interviews and recording sessions, and many bottles of wine were also consumed in the process. There had also been some financial outlay on my part. The years went by and as I was not yet seeing the fruits of this arrangement, or effort, I began to become concerned at the lack of progress.

Eventually, mainly because my youngest brother, Mike, had planned a trip to the UK and I wanted to coincide publication with his visit, I began to put increased pressure on my ghost writer to produce the goods. This all happened three to four years ago now. I was given promise after promise and none of these promises were ever met with any productive delivery of words. I began to increase the pressure and words did start to appear except that they were not the words of my ghost writer, they were simply a transcript of some of the interviews. It was rubbish. I progressively began to realise that the only way that my memoirs were going to be written was if I wrote them myself. In July 2017, I sacked my publisher friend as the author of my book and made the decision to write the book myself. However, I first wanted to find a new publisher. About the only thing that my first 'publisher' had got right was a name for the book. I had originally thought of a suitable title along the line of *Always Supersonic*. That was until I was speaking to my good friend, John Hutchinson, a retired Concorde pilot and also a fellow past master of the Honourable Company of Air Pilots. He said to me, "Come on, Rick, you can't call it that. You guys were only supersonic for minutes, we were supersonic for hours!" I immediately thought to myself that John had a point and that was the end of my first idea. It was my publisher contact who came up with the idea to call the book *Rate of Climb* to reflect the performance of the Lightning fighter, my favourite aircraft, and also to reflect on a successful career.

In October 2018, I attended the book launch in the RAF Club of Sir Richard Johns' autobiography which was being published by Grub Street Publishing. I had previously met John Davies from Grub Street and I touched base with him that evening. He was interested, we met and I was delighted when he said that he would take on the task. Now, I just had to write the book and I won't say that I didn't find the initial timescale challenging, mainly because of the many other things in which I was, and am, involved.

Another reason why I decided to write the book was because there are years in my father's life that, to this day, I know little about. His parents, my paternal grandparents died before I was born and so I have missed that part of my family upbringing. Over the years I found myself increasingly thirsty for knowledge about my ancestry which I found difficult to obtain. I decided there and then that I wanted to leave a written legacy for my own children, my grandchildren and, for that matter, for any future descendants. They will be able to read what their ancestor, me, had done in my life.

At this point I would also like to record that, for anyone who reads this book in years to come, there are at least two other places that hold significant information about mainly my career but also with reference to my life. I was called by a historian from the Imperial War Museum early in 2019 who said to me, "Rick, I have been given your name as someone whose life we should record for the IWM archives, are you interested?" To which I replied, "Yes, I certainly am". I thought that this would be something like a two-hour interview and so his next comment came as surprise, "That is great, Rick. It should take no longer than about twelve two-hour interviews"! Well, that is exactly how long it took and the IWM now holds about 24 hours of interview time with me about my life and career. However, the material is not allowed to be used until I am no longer on this planet. The RAF Museum also hold in their archives a two-hour interview with me about my RAF career.

I am pleased that I have persevered with this book over a period covering many years, and I will add that when I have got deep into the written word,

I have enjoyed the experience because it has brought back so many happy memories in the process.

I am left with a feeling that I have not written in sufficient detail about my own family, and how much they mean to me – all the places where we have lived, the birth of my three children – I was present at all three births, an unforgettable experience – and their growing-up years, their time at their schools, Lockers Park Prep School for Ian, Berkhamsted Girls for Lisa and Jenny and then Bradfield College for all three. Also, I need to give recognition to the fact that Lisa got a scholarship to Bradfield. Then there are the holidays that we have enjoyed, to South Africa on many occasions to see my family, holidays with the Holiday Property Bond (HPB), both overseas and in the UK, all very enjoyable holidays.

Of special mention must be my 70th birthday celebrations in 2015. I thought to myself where did I want to celebrate my 70th birthday and the answer was simple. I wanted to have all of my family with me but, most importantly, I wanted to celebrate the milestone with my brothers. We had had such a happy upbringing together and there was only just over three years between the three of us. It was an opportune occasion, and also timely, because it was not only the last time that we had the whole family together in South Africa but it was also the last time that I saw my middle brother, John, who died just a few months later, in May 2015.

My wife, Tina, deserves a whole book written about her. She has supported me through thick and thin, and she has been a fantastic mother and grand-mother. She herself is a very special person to whom I owe a debt of gratitude. Most importantly, she has now put up with all my foibles for 46 years!

I have made no mention until now of what I will call a very special group of people who, for many years, shared some really very special holidays. That group comprises myself and Tina, Chris and Ro Davison, Cliff and Caroline Spink and Jim and Kathy Uprichard. The boys are all old RAF colleagues and the girls have also known each other for many years. Importantly, we are all members of an excellent holiday organisation, the Holiday Property Bond. Every year for over ten years we all went on holiday together to one of the top-quality HPB properties, usually to an overseas European location. These holidays were always full of sport, sightseeing, fun, banter and pure enjoyment. Memorable holidays with special people.

I am sure that there is still much that I have forgotten. If anyone feels aggrieved that they have not had a mention, please let me know and we will see how we can address the matter in the future.

I hope *Rate of Climb* has given you a good insight into my first 75 years on planet earth. It has been wonderful in every way. I have been blessed with loving parents and the company of my two brothers. In flying and aviation in general, I was fortunate to find my niche in life. My experiences have been multi-varied and memorable. I have travelled the world and I cherish many great friendships. I hope you have enjoyed reading about some of my adventures and I look forward to writing my next book. *Per Ardua Ad Astra.*

INDEX